BMW

MOTORCYCLES

THE EVOLUTION OF EXCELLENCE

BMW

MOTORCYCLES

THE EVOLUTION OF EXCELLENCE

KEVIN ASH

Whitehorse Press
Center Conway, New Hampshire

Whitehorse Press books are also available at discounts in bulk quantity for sales and promotional use. For details about special sales or for a catalog of motorcycling books, videos, and gear write to the publisher:

Whitehorse Press
107 East Conway Road
Center Conway, New Hampshire 03813
Phone: 603-356-6556 or 800-531-1133
E-mail: CustomerService@WhitehorsePress.com
Internet: www.WhitehorsePress.com

ISBN-13: 978-1-884313-57-8
ISBN-10: 1-884313-57-4

5 4 3 2 1

Printed in China

ACKNOWLEDGEMENTS

The author gratefully acknowledges the permission granted by BMW Group and BMW Mobile Tradition for use of images from their company archives. Those organizations supplied all images used in this book, except for the following, which were supplied by the author:

pages 5, 30, 129, 146, 150, 157, 162, 165, and 174.

The author would also like to acknowledge the role of Fred Jakobs, historian and archivist for BMW Mobile Tradition in Munich, who read through the text and applied his encyclopedic knowledge in making some welcomed corrections and suggestions.

Finally, special thanks go to Laurence Kuykendall at BMW North America, whose vision to share the remarkable story of his dynamic company and its superlative motorcycles made this book possible.

Contents

1917 *through* 1945

Between the wars, an ideology is established

During the last century more than 3000 motorcycle companies were founded. Just a few dozen make bikes today, and of those formed before World War II, only a small handful are still in existence. BMW is one of this elite group, and a look at the German company's long and fascinating history shows its survival is not due to the vagaries of fortune, but a unique combination of guiding principles which established it firmly, helped it grow, restricted it, and in the last decade, set it on the road to the most successful period in its history: today!

By the end of 2005 BMW will have produced around 1.8 million motorcycles since its first machine, the R32, was built in 1923. This is an incredible 82 years of near-continuous production, interrupted only by World War II, during which BMW's world motorcycle markets have undergone a series of dramatic changes as economic and political circumstances affected what people wanted or could afford to buy. At one stage BMW was even told what it was and wasn't allowed to make. Of those thousands of other motorcycle factories which have come and gone in this time, some were just unfortunate victims of circumstance, but many others weren't able to adapt their designs or engineering to suit the changing world around them. Yet BMW is not only still here, it entered the new millennium as one of the fastest growing and most promising motorcycle companies in the world.

Attributing BMW's survival to any single factor would be simplistic, but the roots of its strengths lie in the aviation industry where it was founded. Indeed, the creator of the first BMW, Max Friz, was an aircraft engine designer first, in charge of the design department of Daimler engine company from 1906 until 1916, and Rapp Motorenwerke in 1917. This aero engine company became Bayerische Motoren Werke that same year—Bavarian Engine Company. The company's first product was the aero engine BMW IIIa, designed by Max Friz. The IIIa was very successful in WW I because it didn't lose as much power at high altitude as other engines.

After World War I BMW was forbidden by the Treaty of Versailles from building the aero engines it had been created to do (the BMW badge dates

Max Friz designed the first BMW, the R32.

from World War I and represents the Bavarian colors white and blue, later interpreted as a spinning propeller. But Friz's passion was aircraft; before the ban he created the aero engine BMW IV, successor to the high-altitude engine BMW III a. Powered by this new engine, BMW achieved the world altitude record of just over 32,000 feet in 1919. The Allies were deeply unhappy with this, confiscating the plans and insisting that BMW look at other outlets for its production facilities. BMW cast around for something else to busy its engineering workers and equipment and by 1921 was producing the M2B15 fore-and-aft boxer engine as a proprietary motorcycle power unit, used by many other manufacturers, and developed by Martin Stolle from what was originally a British Douglas design. But sales fell as customers began to produce their own motors, and Friz was asked to produce a complete BMW motorcycle. He was reluctant but had little choice; once working on

< The record-breaking BMW IV aero engine of 1919 was also designed by Max Friz.

Martin Stolle developed the M2B15 494cc fore-and-aft boxer twin engine.

the project, he applied himself with the same skill and professionalism as in his aircraft design. The development work done on the M2B15 was paying dividends too, as Friz used all he'd learned, combined with his own ideas, to produce the classic transverse boxer twin which powered the R32 of 1923. This was the very first motorcycle to be called a BMW.

Friz had already recognized the excellent low vibration qualities of the boxer twin and by turning the motor 90 degrees in the frame he improved cylinder cooling, where the rear would easily overheat with the fore-and-aft configuration. The new layout's longitudinal crankshaft also facilitated the use of shaft final drive. As well as looking at the overall architecture of the bike, Friz and Stolle concentrated on dealing with the many reliability problems endemic in so many contemporary machines. By 1923 only the English company ABC had built a motorcycle with a boxer engine

> *BMW's first motorcycle was the R32.*

positioned with transverse cylinders, while the use of a shaft to drive the rear wheel had been attempted by FN in Belgium in 1904. Yet, as with all the best ideas, that combination seems so obviously right in retrospect. Thus the R32 was unique in its design, and thanks to Friz's aero design practices and the company's aircraft-standard manufacturing equipment, the bike went on to gain a reputation for outstanding reliability. It even looked good! It was an expensive bike to make, but its qualities justified the premium price and BMW comfortably established itself at the top end of the market, a region it has inhabited ever since.

Claiming this engine and transmission layout for itself has undoubtedly been one of the factors behind BMW's continued existence, as it has worked so well in so many applications across the decades. But at least as important was the way BMW built the R32: with a level of quality and reliability that were high, without becoming unprofitable or impossibly expensive.

Details have changed beyond recognition since that debut boxer twin of course: the first versions had only a wedge-block rear brake, while the 486cc engine (increased to 494cc in 1925) produced just 8.5 bhp at a lowly 3300 rpm. The top speed of more than 60 mph was respectable enough though. From 1923 until production ceased in 1926, BMW built 3,100 R32s at its Munich factory, where each motorcycle was assembled from start to finish by the same small team.

As we've already seen there is more to BMW than simply an engine layout. Even in the 1920s there were more engine layouts to BMW, although it should be said the 247cc R39 of 1925, BMW's first single, was effectively still half a boxer twin with the cylinder moved upright—the 68mm x 68mm bore and stroke, along with its design and build quality principles, were shared with the R32.

*Each R32 was assembled from start
to finish by a small team.*

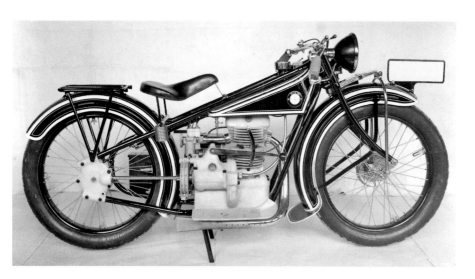

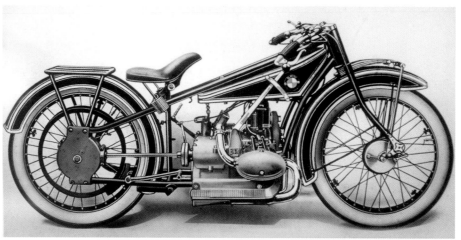

Performance of the R39 was strong, with a power of 6 bhp at 4000 rpm and a 62 mph top speed but, as with the R32, its real strength was the way it was built, which gave it a reputation for exceptional reliability.

Already in these first machines we find two traits which have been associated with BMW throughout its history. The first is outstanding build quality, which although it might have faltered at times, has certainly and importantly been perceived as a BMW trait. The second is innovation, mostly in engineering but also on occasion in concepts themselves. Unfairly this hasn't always been the public perception of BMW, which to many motorcyclists is seen as one of the more conservative companies. Yet innovation has kept the company at the forefront of motorcycle design, and there's no question that it still does, even today.

< The 247cc R39 of 1925 was BMW's first single. Power was 6 bhp at 4000 rpm and top speed was 62 mph.

< The R37 of 1925 was the racing derivative of the R32. Just 152 were made in two years of production.

In so many ways then, the R32 encapsulated from the outset what BMW was to be all about: a boxer twin of course, but also a high quality machine in both design and build. And in another habit that has kept BMW ahead of the game, the R32 began a program of refinement and development as soon as it made its debut. But what surprises those whose experience of BMW is only of more recent machines is the company's extensive activity in competition and record breaking, something which began almost immediately after production started of the R37, the racing derivative of the R32. The R37 was little more than a tuned R32 with the road equipment removed (equipment such as lights, although lights were an option anyway!). It also featured overhead valves and an aluminum cylinder head in place of the R32's side-valve, cast iron head design. It also had an expanding shoe front brake (the same brake used on the R32 since the summer of 1924), and it made 16

bhp, all of which was very advanced for the time. Only 152 were built in two years of production.

During the 1920s and 1930s the value of competition was enormous—much more than now—as a way of proving reliability as much as performance, since reliability was a major issue on all types of vehicle in the 1920s and 1930s. And sure enough, the R37 was highly successful on the track, winning around 100 events in Germany alone in 1925, including the 500cc class of the German Grand Prix.

> The R37 was a great success in competition, winning around 100 events in Germany alone in 1925. Performance was helped by the addition of an expanding shoe front brake.

But winning foreign competitions against home-grown machines was the best way of generating the most high-profile headlines, and a very effective one for introducing a new name in potential export markets, so the company put much effort into these. BMW's engineer Rudolf Schleicher (later head of the motorcycle development and racing department) won BMW's first major international trophy on an R37, taking a gold medal in the International Six Days Trial (ISDT) in Wales in 1926, then considered the toughest event in motorcycle sport. The only other BMW in the race was ridden by a friend of Schleicher, who won a silver medal and helped to power BMW into the public's attention in the UK. Then, over the following three years, it was the Italians' turn to taste humility, when the German marque won the terrifyingly tough Targa Florio three times in succession with Paul Köppen, followed by Ernst Henne in 1928, then Köppen again. The UK and

The famous Targa Florio is where BMW proved the value of supercharging its twins. Paul Köppen is pictured here in 1929 on his number 2 machine on the start line before making it a third win for BMW.

< BMW's chief test engineer Rudolf Schleicher won BMW's first major trophy on this R37. The bike produced 16 bhp at 4000 rpm, almost double the R32's power.

Ernst Henne collected 76 world records between 1929 and 1937. He's pictured here in 1929 setting the mile record at 134.68 mph on a supercharged 750 on the road between Munich and Ingolstadt.

Italy were the world's most significant motorcycle producers at the time, so getting noticed in either was a major achievement.

Henne holds a special place in BMW's history. In the 1920s and 1930s breaking world records was another very effective way of generating lots of publicity, and Henne was undoubtedly BMW's most successful exponent of this activity, collecting 76 records between 1929 and 1937. He started by gaining the one-mile record at 134.68 mph on a supercharged 750 twin—BMW was to become a major pioneer of supercharging, with a great deal of practical research being carried out on Henne's machines. Henne's passion for records even extended to ice racing: in 1930 he was competing on a supercharged 500 twin fitted with studded ice tires! He spent much of the following year attempting to reclaim his world mile record from Joe Wright, on a 745cc Kompressor (kompressor is German for supercharger). Wright had topped the

Ernst Henne raced on the ice in 1930 on the supercharged 500cc twin modified with studded tires.

Ernst Henne in 1931 aboard a 750 Kompressor on the Munich-Ingolstadt road attempted to reclaim his world record from Joe Wright. Henne finally beat Wright in 1932 with a 151.77 mph pass.

Ernst Henne, at Gyon in Hungary in 1934, raised his own previous record of 151.77 mph to 152.81 mph on a 745cc Kompressor twin.

> Here is Josef Selzer on the R39 racer at the German Solitude circuit in 1926.

German's previous record but Henne finally beat him in 1932, then raised the record again to 152.81 mph on another 745cc Kompressor twin in 1934. He carried on breaking records until 1937 and remained unbeaten until 1951.

Josef Selzer meanwhile won the German 250cc championship in 1925 on a racing version of the R39 single, and was very successful in 1926 on the same machine. He became instrumental not just in proving the R39's performance and reliability but, with his subsequent successes on bikes such as the R47, was another rider who helped to establish BMW as a major manufacturer. The R47, produced in 1927, was a sports oriented machine, superseding the R37—it kept the outgoing bike's leaf spring front suspension and overhead valves, but power was increased by 2 bhp to an impressive 18 bhp at 4000 rpm. Over the next two years, 1,720 machines were sold, a useful number at the time.

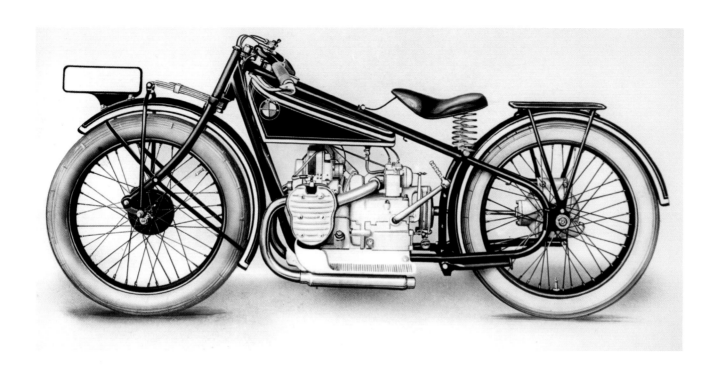

The R42 superseded the R32. Power was increased to
12 bhp at 3400 rpm and the rear block brake was
replaced by a drive-shaft shoe brake.

< The sports R47 of 1927 was the sporting option,
superseding the R37. Power was increased by 2 bhp
to 18 bhp at 4000 rpm.

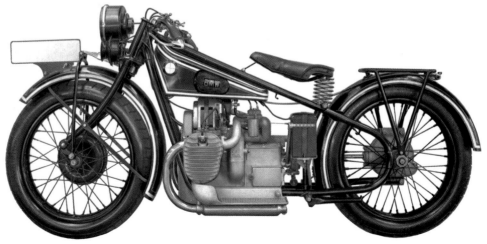

The R32 road bike was superseded in 1926 by the R42; more an evolution than a new model, the R42 reflected lessons learned from the R37 race machine. This model development policy was and still is typical of BMW: gentle evolution supplemented now and again by sudden and sometimes sweeping model changes. The R42's power was raised to 12 bhp at 3400 rpm, and improved efficiency also helped fuel consumption. A drive-shaft shoe brake replaced the old block-type, but lights were still an option!

The first production BMW 750 was the 745cc R62 of 1928, a touring bike rather than sports machine with a side-valve engine producing 18 bhp at 3400 rpm. The pistons were still being made of cast iron at the time, although the sporting R63 derivative which arrived later in the year used aluminum pistons.

The R63 was the first BMW to be tagged the 'Golden Arrow' by the British and American press

< The R52 of 1928 replaced the R42. It used the same 78mm stroke as the R62 with a 63mm bore. Capacity was 487cc capacity with a power output of 12 bhp at 3400 rpm.

< The first production BMW 750 was the 745cc R62 of 1928, with a side-valve engine producing 18 bhp at 3400 rpm.

The 745cc R11 was distinguished by its pressed steel frame. BMWs with these frames were known as 'star framed' bikes. In the early 1930s, several German manufacturers built bikes with pressed steel frames—and boxer engines. The press came to identify this design as the "German School of Motorcycles."

for its high performance, a name that carried over to the R16 that followed. The R63 was significantly changed from the R62: as well as new pistons, it had overhead valves and oversquare bore and stroke dimensions of 83mm x 63mm. Power was 24 bhp at 4000 rpm, impressive for a road bike at the time.

The 487cc R52 arrived the same year, taking over from the R42 and maintaining BMW's relentless development pace. The R52 was simply a smaller version of the R62, using the same 78mm stroke with smaller 63mm pistons, unusually undersquare dimensions for BMW which were responsible for the much lower power of just 12 bhp at 3400 rpm. Lower sidecar gearing was an option, and with that came with a stronger double-plate clutch.

And the development pace kept on going: just one year later, in 1929, the R62 supplemented the 745cc R11, a bike distinctive for its pressed steel frame, used because it was cheaper to produce. It wasn't a popular look, although BMWs with these frames were known as 'star framed' bikes, probably a corruption of the German 'stark' meaning strong, and they were considered tough at least. Power was still 18 bhp, but top speed only 62 mph. Only a few of these bikes were sold before they went into full production in 1931. Oh yes, and lights were standard, at last.

The pace at which new models were being developed and upgraded was as hot as in any of the modern bike categories today, which comes as a real surprise to those who might have expected the 1920s and 1930s to be an altogether gentler time. But remember that the technology was young and, just as with computers in the last two decades, it was a time of rapid progress; any company that didn't keep the pressure on would fall behind rapidly. The driving force behind BMW's relentless model development was Franz Josef

Franz Josef Popp's vision and leadership were the forces behind the creation of BMW's young and dynamic team of engineers, and it was his idea to apply aerospace standards to motorcycles.

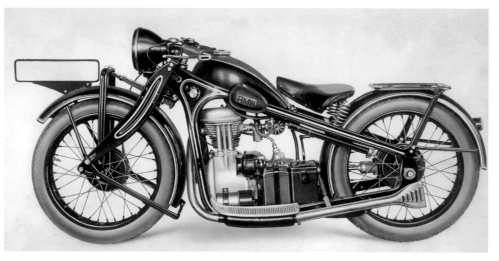

Popp, who joined the company in 1917, and soon became general manager, thanks to his engineering background and management skills. His vision and leadership were the catalyst behind the creation of BMW's young and dynamic team of engineers. It had been his idea to apply aerospace engineering standards to motorcycles, although without a man the caliber of Friz to apply them, it would have been difficult to achieve. Equally important, the demand for aero engines was not constant over time. They might have an order to produce 200 engines in four weeks, and then have no orders for the next two months. BMW entered the motorcycle business partly to provide work for its highly skilled workforce. The same engineers, workers, and machines were used to make aero engines and motorcycles.

Even so, like any other manufacturer with reasonable business sense, BMW's models were by necessity a product of their times, in economic as

< The smallest BMW of the 20th century, the 198cc R2, was introduced in 1931 (1932 model shown), to dip under a German 200cc tax limit. It was also the upper limit for bikes that could be ridden without a license.

< The star-framed 'Golden Arrow' R16 was the sporting stablemate of the R11, featuring a 736cc overhead valve, 83mm x 68mm engine making 25 bhp at 4000 rpm. Weight was up 10kg (22 lb) to 165kg (364 lb) compared to the old R63.

well as fashion terms. With the world in recession at the beginning of the 30s, large capacity motorcycles were luxuries few could afford, so in 1931 BMW proved its flexibility by producing its smallest motorcycle of the 20th century, the 198cc R2, a bike designed to slot into a German 200cc tax bracket. Even BMW couldn't ignore the dominance of the utility bike market and weakness of the other classes, although the R2 was still expensive compared with budget offerings from other manufacturers—a budget bike, but unmistakably a BMW budget bike. Not that tight financial restrictions hindered innovation: the overhead valve, 6 bhp engine was the first BMW with a one-piece 'tunnel' crankcase, a design which enhanced strength and reliability while reducing production costs.

The R11 meanwhile, with its low-cost pressed-steel frame, was still being made and of course being developed. Even as it reached the end of its production life the single SUM carburetor was replaced with twin Amals, raising power 2 bhp to 20 bhp—the pursuit of performance was still important, even in that class at that time!

Twin Amals were also fitted to the R16 (on the mark 5 version), another star-framed machine. This was the sporting partner of the R11, on sale alongside it but pitched at a different market sector. It had a 736cc overhead valve engine producing 25 bhp at 4000 rpm, but weight was up 22 lb

> *The 1935 R7 had full monocoque bodywork and was the first BMW to be fitted with telescopic front forks, but the machine was thought too radical to go into production.*

> *The R12 was a milestone in motorcycle history as the first production bike to be fitted with telescopic front forks, patented by BMW.*

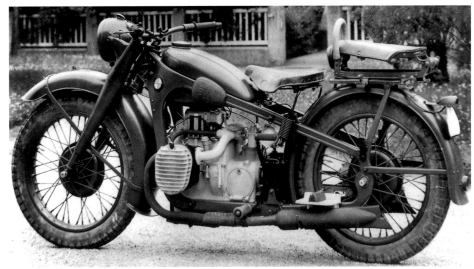

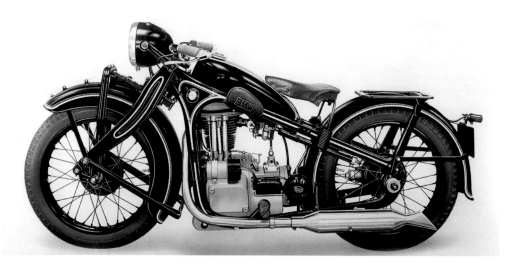

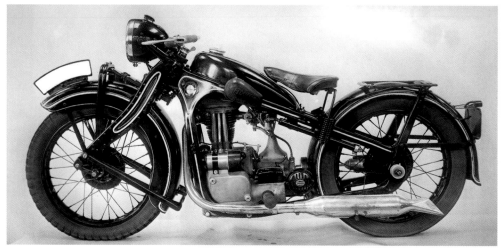

over the old R63 to 364 lb. As mentioned, this too was dubbed 'Golden Arrow' as the replacement for the R63, which it justified with 75 mph performance.

BMW's engineers were busy experimenting still, and extended the pressed steel frame concept a dramatic step further with the 1935 R7, which had full monocoque bodywork supporting the steering head and rear axle. The bike was also notable as the first BMW to be fitted with telescopic front forks, but the machine was considered too radical to be a sales success and never went into production. The telescopic fork was tested intensively in 1934 in all kinds of motorsports: on the factory road racing bike with the early tubular frame, on the ISDT works team bikes (based on the R16), and on Ernst Henne's sidecar record-breaker for Gyon in Hungary. Winning the Six Days Trials earned great publicity for telescopic forks.

< The rugged 398cc single-cylinder R4 was made for the military, hence the right-side kick start, unusual for BMW. The bike gained a four-speed gearbox in 1933 and power was increased by 2 bhp to 14 bhp for this 1935 series 4 model, although top speed was still a modest 65 mph.

< The R3 of 1936 was closely based on the single-cylinder R4, its 305cc capacity achieved by reducing the bore to 68mm from the R4's 78mm. The stroke of 84mm was retained, as was the rolling chassis. Power and top speed were good at 11 bhp and 62 mph, but sales were poor and only 740 were made in the one year of production.

The distinction of first production motorcycle to be fitted with telescopic forks went to the R12, a milestone in motorcycling history, let alone BMW's. There was no doubt that racing was improving the breed as well as publicizing it, as telescopic forks had been tested, refined, and proven on the tracks first. Now the R12 brought telescopic forks to a much wider and highly appreciative audience. The idea of telescopic forks became spoils of war for the Allies after WW II, when BMW's patents would have otherwise seriously handicapped rival manufacturers, so superior were they to any contemporary alternatives.

The tough pre-war economic climate meanwhile dictated the continued production of more prosaic machines alongside the R12, and from 1932 to 1938 around 15,000 examples of the rugged 398cc single-cylinder R4 were made, many for the military. This is why the bike featured a right-side kick start, unusual for BMW but a prerequisite for army motorcycles, as most soldiers are right-handed and often need to dismount to start a left-kickstart machine. This can be difficult on rough terrain, and might cost life-saving seconds. The R4 was upgraded with a four-speed gearbox in 1933 and power was increased by 2 bhp to 14 bhp for the 1935 series 4 model, although top speed was still a modest 65 mph. But even this didn't escape the development program.

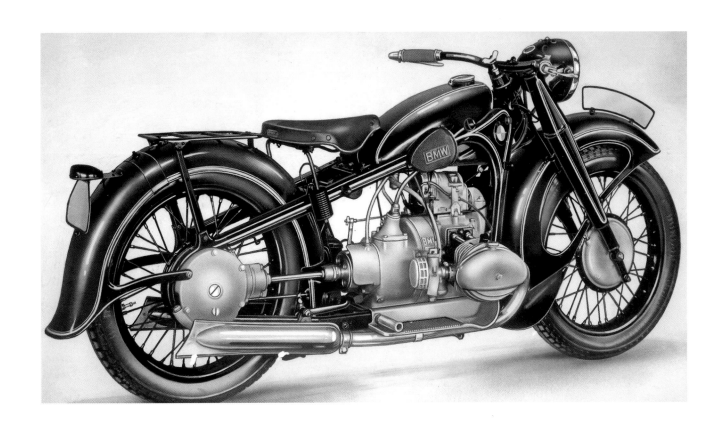

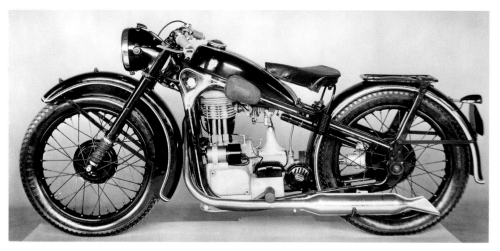

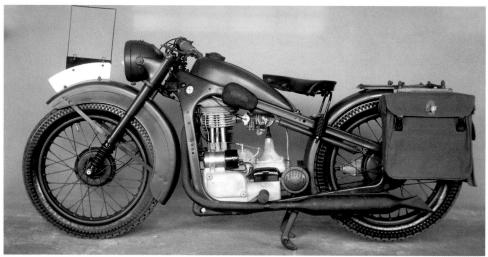

BMW's engineering was based on sound principles, and it tried hard to get its nomenclature to follow suit. Hence a lot of early models' names reflected their engine capacities: the R4 was 400cc, and the later R5 and R6 twins were 500cc and 600cc respectively. This explains why the 1936 R3 superseded the R4, even if the numbers look like the reverse: the R3 was closely based on the R4 in fact, its 305cc capacity achieved by reducing the bore 10mm to 68mm. The stroke and rolling chassis were unchanged. Power and top speed were good at 11 bhp and 62 mph but, because the R3 had neither the low price of the R2 nor the power of the R4 (which was only slightly more expensive), sales were poor and only 740 R3s were made in its single year of production.

The R12 wasn't the only production BMW with telescopic forks in 1935, as like many previous models it was complemented by a sporting alternative—in this case the R17. Other advanced

< In 1937 the R4 was replaced with the 342cc R35. Although the R35 now featured telescopic forks and fashionable 19-inch wheels, this civilian version was designed so that few changes were needed in order to appeal to the conservative military. The R35 also saw a small power increase over the old R4, up to 14 bhp at 4500 rpm despite the 4mm reduction in bore to 72mm, while top speed was unchanged at 62 mph.

< The majority of the 15,000 R35s made during its three-year production run from 1937 were military. For this reason the bike retained the old-fashioned hand-shift, four-speed gearbox with right-side kickstart and sprung saddle.

features on the bike included interchangeable 19-inch wheels, a four-speed gearbox and twin Amal carburetors (a British design made in Germany under license). The overhead valve, 736cc 33 bhp engine revved up to 5000 rpm and the bike's top speed was 87 mph. The old R16's rigid rear end star frame was still deemed good enough though, an odd contrast with the world leading front end design!

Meanwhile, in the bread-and-butter sector, the sluggish-selling R3 was soon replaced by the 342cc R35, which apart from its telescopic forks and fashionable 19-inch wheels wasn't greatly changed as it still had to appeal to the notoriously conservative military. Power was up slightly to 14 bhp at 4500 rpm despite the 4mm reduction in bore to 72mm, while the top speed was un-changed at 62 mph. It was a sign of the times, with tension building in Europe, that the majority of the 15,000 R35s made during its three-year

> *The innovative 1936 R5 was one of the great bikes of its decade. Features included telescopic forks, a steering damper, and positive stop foot gearshift. The advanced, all-new 494cc engine was now twin-cam with a one-piece tunnel crankcase. Power was 24 bhp at 5800 rpm. Shown is the 1937 version.*

> *In 1938 the plunger rear suspension developed on the race machines was added to the R5—the bike was renamed the R51.*

production run from 1937 were military and police rather than civilian versions. It was for this reason alone, pandering to the army's very cautious thinking, that the bike still retained the by now old-fashioned hand-change, four-speed gearbox with right-side kickstart and sprung saddle.

It's a tribute to BMW's dynamic engineering team therefore that with such stale-thinking demands on the one hand, they could simultaneously produce one of the most advanced bikes of the decade—indeed, one of the greatest. The innovative 1936 R5 had a range of cutting edge features including telescopic forks, a steering damper and, making its BMW debut, a positive-stop foot gear shift. This is the same gear shift system we use today, 70 years later, a design invented by Harold Willis for the English company Velocette in 1928. While it must have hurt BMW's pride to take on-board a foreign invention, its advantages were overwhelming. The Germans were

< The 1937 R6 was the side-valve version of the R5, aimed more at sidecar users, and it shared the R5's rolling chassis and much of the engine and transmission, although new bore and stroke dimensions of 69.8mm x 78mm meant capacity increased to 596.9cc. Power was 18 bhp.

< Like the R5, the R6 became the R61 with the addition of rear suspension.

A wing nut adjusts the rod-operated rear drum brake on the 192cc 1937 R20. Note the frame is now tubular steel but still there is no rear suspension. Even the telescopic front forks were crude, doing without hydraulic damping, while the foot-operated gearchange was not positive stop, meaning gears could be selected in any order.

at least quicker to adopt it than many other manufacturers. The R5's twin cradle frame meanwhile was astonishingly high tech, featuring tubular steel with an exotic combination of round and oval sections joined by electric and gas welding, and chosen according to the loads they had to deal with. The all-new 24 bhp 494cc engine was advanced too, now with twin cams, a one-piece tunnel crankcase and a rev ceiling of more than 6000 rpm—this was before World War II! The sophistication of the R5 was enhanced further in 1938 with the addition of plunger rear suspension, developed originally on BMW's race machines. The rear axle was mounted onto telescopic shock absorbers built onto the rear end of the frame, allowing about two inches of movement. The bike was renamed the R51, although the plunger rear suspension was its only significant change from the R5.

The 192cc R20 in 1938 was replaced by the R23, the main difference being an 8mm increase in bore size to 68mm to give 247cc.

The 1938 597cc R66 shared the R51's rolling chassis and transmission. The engine used a single camshaft and the side-valve twin's crankcases along with overhead valves and was the quickest production BMW to date. Its 30 bhp engine was good for a top speed of 90 mph.

The R71 replaced the R12 in 1938. Peak output was just 22 bhp at 4600 rpm, but the low-power, high-torque engine was meant primarily for sidecar use and cruising on the new Autobahn roads. This was BMW's last side-valve engine.

For all the glamour and status of bikes like the R5, the Bavarian factory was still keeping its commercial eye focused, and in 1937 the R6 made its debut, a more utilitarian alternative with a sidevalve engine aimed mostly at sidecar users. It shared the R5's rolling chassis, which reduced costs, and much of the engine and transmission too, although the new bore and stroke dimensions of 69.8mm x 78mm meant the capacity increased to 596.9cc. Power was a gentle 18 bhp, but low rev torque was substantial, and the R6 label fitted the engine displacement more than 60 years before Yamaha sequestrated the name and near enough the capacity for its middleweight sports bike. Like the R5, the R6 became the R61 in 1938 with the addition of rear suspension. Similarly, the only other changes were concomitant ones, such as the inclusion of a universal joint in the drive shaft and a new bevel drive housing and rear frame design.

Here is Georg Meier at the 1938 TT.

The R5 was workmanlike in concept, but those original principles were still being adhered to: the prices of this and indeed the R6 reflected their quality and sophistication, each costing up to double their equivalents from the British bike industry, which was the biggest in the world at the time. But there was compensation with both machines in exceptional reliability and durability, as well as their superior riding qualities.

Despite this, BMW was still managing to cater for the bottom end of the market profitably, although its labeling had to gain a factor of ten with the 192cc R20, out the same year as the R6. The frame was changed to tubular steel but still there was no rear suspension, and even the apparently modern telescopic front forks were in fact very crude, doing without hydraulic damping, while the foot-operated gearchange was not positive stop, meaning gears could be selected in any order. But it was of course very well made.

> *The dynamic Jock West finished second behind Georg Meier at the Isle of Man TT in 1939.*

1938 was exceptionally busy in Bavaria even by BMW's own standards, and aside from the company building its 100,000th motorcycle that year. First, in response to a new law allowing bikes under 250cc to be tax free, the 192cc R20 was replaced by the R23, although the only significant difference here was an 8mm bigger piston at 68mm to bring the capacity up to 247cc. One other welcome change was the partial recession into the fuel tank of the toolbox, whose prominence on the R20 had caused some eye-watering injuries in sudden stops.

The 597cc R66 was new that year too. This shared the R51's rolling chassis and transmission, but the 30 bhp engine used the old side-valve twin's crankcases combined with a single camshaft and overhead valves, making it the quickest production BMW to date at 90 mph.

The fifth bike to debut in '38 was the R71, a machine designed to replace the old R12. The

< Georg Meier makes his way to an historic Senior TT victory on the supercharged 500 BMW, which averaged 89.38 mph throughout the race. This was the first foreign rider on a foreign machine to ever win the Senior TT.

peak engine output was just 22 bhp at 4600 rpm, but the low power, high torque engine was meant primarily for sidecar use and long-distance cruising on the new Autobahn roads. For the same reason, early versions were also fitted with a hand gear-change, although this was soon replaced with a positive stop foot change, and it was BMW's last side-valve.

While BMW was being prolific in the show-rooms in 1938, it was generally a very successful year on the track too, with three BMW-mounted riders setting the pace. Rising German star Georg Meier won the European Championship, the first year it became a race series rather than a single event, while the factory offered strong support to Jock West, the British BMW importer's sales man-ager, even loaning him a factory bike and mechan-ics for some races as he campaigned effectively in the UK. But 1938 wasn't BMW's year at the Isle of Man TT, then the greatest prize in motorcycle racing: BMW's third ace this year, Karl Gall, crashed out in practice while Meier's bike was left on the start line after a spark plug thread stripped. The non-supercharged 500cc race bike he used this and the following year featured plunger-type rear suspension, introduced on the race bikes in 1937. It was very quick: even with twin carbure-tors instead of a supercharger, top speed was around 120 mph.

But come 1939 and BMW did the unthinkable, winning the Isle of Man Senior TT, the most presti-gious of all international motorcycle races and one which had only ever been won on a British bike by British riders. Meier circulated the daunting 37-3/4

> *BMW also designed the 14-cylinder radial engine which powered the Focke-Wulf 190 fighter of 1942.*

mile island course at a race average speed of 89.38 mph, his pre-war, unfaired (fairings were forbidden by the racing rules), and now supercharged machine exceeding 140 mph at times. The bike was thought to produce around 70 bhp, a colossal amount of power for the time.

In 1939 the world changed forever with the onset of World War II. BMW focused now on designing and building aero engines, a business it had continued building after 1924, and which had produced six-cylinder inline, V-12, and radial engines. One of its best known engines included the 14-cylinder radial which powered the Focke-Wulf 190 fighter of 1942. With its 410 mph top speed and 37,000 feet ceiling it outperformed the British Spitfire. The company also became an early pioneer in jet engine design and production. A prototype engine called the 003 was running as early as 1942 and went into full production in 1943, although Allied bombing of the Munich factory

< During WW II BMW became an early pioneer in jet engine design and production. This prototype engine, called the 003, was running as early as 1942. BMW was the first company to bring jet engines to production standards.

The R75 of 1942 was produced for the military, and some 18,000 were made up to 1944.

caused serious disruption. By that stage in the war more than 35,000 people were working for BMW.

Motorcycle production continued too, now directed at the war effort. The R75 was produced solely for the military, and some 18,000 were made up to 1944. The bike had four forward gears and one reverse, combined with a low-ratio box for off-road use, and an overhead-valve, single-cam 745cc engine. The bike was almost always fitted with a sidecar whose wheel was driven through a lock-up differential. The 16-inch wheels were interchangeable and could take car tires. Performance inevitably was sluggish as a fully equipped R75 outfit could weigh half a ton and the engine only made 26 bhp, but thanks to plenty of low rev torque it was effective in mud and sand.

From 1942 the R75's air filter was mounted on top of the fuel tank to keep it clear of dirt and sand. This was also the year motorcycle production moved from Munich to Eisenach, previously BMW's car factory, while Munich was given over solely to the production of aero engines. After the war this hindered the restarting of motorcycle production, as Eisenach fell under Soviet control while Munich was in the control of the Americans.

But despite the move and the state of war, a factor common to every R75 was the astonishing dependabililly—the bikes kept on running in the most appalling conditions, while being subjected to the most rudimentary maintenance and dreadful quality of fuel and oil.

> *The R75 was almost always fitted with a sidecar, whose wheel was driven via a lockable differential. The 16-inch wheels were interchangeable and could take car tires.*

1945 *through* 1956

Recovery and a return to growth

After the war BMW was first banned from motor-cycle manufacture, then it was given a 60cc limit, which it didn't take up. In 1948 the limit was raised to 250cc. This suited the single-cylinder R24, an updated R23. Because the production drawings had been lost to the Soviets when they took over BMW's Eisenach motorcycle factory after the war, BMW had to reconstruct the drawings by disassembling an R23 and redrawing each part. As with all BMW singles until the F650 in the 1990s, the R24 had its crank aligned along the bike. It had a dry, single-plate clutch mounted on the back, to suit shaft final drive. The R25 superseded this in 1950, the main change being plunger rear

> *After the war BMW produced the single-cylinder R24, an updated R23. The crank was aligned along the bike with the dry, single-plate clutch mounted on the back.*

suspension, which appeared for the first time on a BMW single. The engine was the same (12 bhp at 5600 rpm), but performance was slightly down as the chassis changes came with a 22 lb weight penalty.

BMW was concentrating on the lowest cost utility transport, for which there was huge demand in the immediate post-war years. Even so, the Germans still couldn't bring themselves to drop their traditional standards: a cheap BMW cost at least 50 percent more than a cheap BSA! It might seem like an odd policy in the face of post-war austerity, but just as many companies weren't able to produce bikes of the same high quality as BMW, so it was equally true that BMW didn't know how to make bikes more cheaply than it did. This is not a facetious observation. BMW had just come through a war—in which the pace of research and development is inevitably accelerated—where it stood at the forefront of aviation technology. All

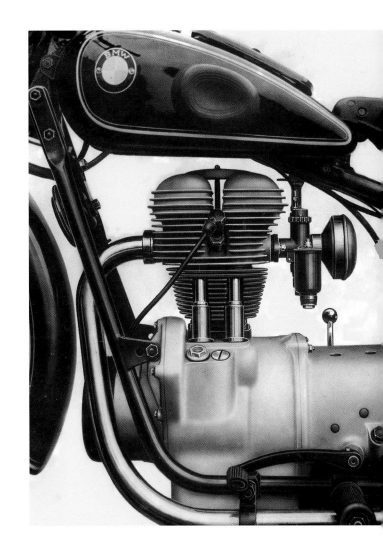

its engineers were trained to aerospace standards, and this after a quarter century of producing premium quality motorcycles. The ethic, the factory, the equipment, and the workforce were all geared to fabricating a high quality product, whatever it might be, and even if BMW had made a conscious policy decision to compete with the cheapest mass

> *The R67 of 1951 was the first really new twin produced after the war, although the R51/2 went on sale after hostilities ceased as an updated prewar R51. The R67's 594cc engine used a gear-driven single camshaft and was generally modernized and tidied.*

This shot of an R25 in Pisa was originally taken privately but when sent to the factory was used by the marketing department in a sales brochure! Note the 'rising BMW' badge on the front fender. The R25 was essentially an R24 fitted with plunger rear suspension, the first on a BMW single. The engine was the same overhead valve, 68mm x 68mm bore and stroke unit producing 12 bhp at 5600 rpm, but performance was slightly down as the changes came with a 10kg weight penalty.

The R51/3 of 1951 had an unprecedented 160 Watt
dynamo (60 Watts was the norm) for vastly improved electrics. The 494cc twin produced 24 bhp at
5800 rpm.

production factories, it simply wouldn't have been very good at it!

The development of brand image half a century ago was not the stuff of spin and manipulation it can be today, but if a company had ever wanted to substantiate its association with quality, it couldn't have done any better than BMW, if only by its pricing policy. But there was substance to back it up—the bikes did last, and they were reliable, more so than most of their many rivals. And therein lies the enormous power of BMW's brand image today: ask anyone to name a high quality motorcycle company and BMW will be at or near the top of most peoples' lists. BMW's reputation for quality derives not just from modern machines, but because the Germans have been building high quality products for so many decades.

This focus on singles to meet the urgent need for personal mobility meant the first new-design post-war twins didn't arrive until 1951. The R51/2

The 1952 R68 was BMW's first 100 mph motorcycle. Its 590cc overhead valve engine produced 35 bhp and revved to more than 7000 rpm.

had gone on sale in 1950 but this was simply a pre-war R51 with some updates, but the R67 was a new, modern machine, followed soon after by the R51/3. These had taken longer to uprate than the singles, and the market for anything other than basic machinery was only then starting to show signs of revival. The R67's 594cc engine used a gear-driven single camshaft and was generally modernized and tidied, but still these were workmanlike machines, designed mostly for sidecar use.

One year later BMW resumed its pursuit of performance once again, as in 1952 the company introduced the R68, its first 100 mph motorcycle. The 590cc overhead valve engine produced 35 bhp and revved beyond 7000 rpm. The bike was available either as a conventional road machine or in 'cross-country' guise, where it was fitted with a high level two-into-one exhaust and dual purpose tires.

The process of continual development hadn't been forgotten during the war either, as the R67 soon became the R67/2 with an assortment of mild upgrades. It too was now available in cross-country guise, with or without a sidecar and with optional electrical equipment. Although the bore and stroke were identical to the R68's 72mm x 73mm, a lower compression ratio and smaller Bing carburetors resulted in a considerably more modest 26 bhp at 5500 rpm.

> *The R67/2 was a slightly upgraded version of the 1951 R67 and, like the R68, was also available as a cross country version, even when fitted with a sidecar. Although the bore and stroke were identical to the R68's 72mm x 73mm, a lower compression ratio with smaller Bing carburetors resulted in a more modest 26 bhp at 5500 rpm. This photo shows a prototype for use by authorities, with additional electrical equipment such as lights and radio.*

The drive for exceptional reliability that was so important to Max Friz in the early 1920s still mattered now to BMW—it was a trait that continued to define the company, giving customers a reason to buy BMW despite the extra cost. So in 1952 the engine of the R51/3 received the same makeover as the R67—ignition now was by magneto, and the 494cc twin's output was up slightly to 24 bhp at 5800 rpm. It was also fitted with an unprecedented 160 watt dynamo (60 watts was the norm) for vastly improved electrics, including a stop light as standard. Lots of effort was also put into keeping the electrics dry to prevent the all too common problems bikes of the time experienced in wet weather.

Nor did the singles escape BMW's mission to improve. In 1953 the R25/3 was uprated substantially, and although power was up only 1 bhp to 13 bhp there was a lot more mid-range torque, which helped endow it with an impressive 74 mph

top speed and improved suitability for sidecar use. The forks now featured rebound as well as compression damping, adding sophistication to the constantly improving reliability.

It looked as though BMW's pre-war racing prowess would not be matched again, not least because of the 1946 ban on supercharging. Some thought this was motivated by a desire to help the British and Italian factories, who lagged behind BMW in this respect, but whatever the reason, the consequence for BMW was having the rug pulled from beneath the feet of its race department. As if that wasn't enough, Germany was banned from international sport, including the 1948 Olympics and 1950 soccer World Cup, although BMW still

> *The 1953 R25/3 was a substantially improved R25. Power was up 1 bhp to 13 bhp with a lot more mid-range torque, and top speed was 74 mph.*

< *Walter Zeller makes his way to victory at the German Grand Prix at Solitude in 1953 on the fuel injected Rennsport 500.*

The 1955 R69 was acclaimed for its blend of performance and sophistication. It was the first road BMW to feature the new Earles-type leading link forks.

The R26 of 1955 was the first BMW single to be fitted with Earles forks. Swingarm rear suspension was fitted at the back.

> The 1955 R50 replaced the R51/3 and received the same engine and chassis improvements—notably the Earles forks—as the contemporary R69. Power of the 494cc twin was up 2 bhp to 24 bhp giving a top speed of 88 mph.

competed in and won many national races and championships at the time.

Into the 1950s the ban was phased out, allowing Walter Zeller to become a major force on the fuel injected Rennsport 500, and later, in 1956, even he was helped by that enduring BMW trait: reliability. Although he didn't win a single race that year, still he came second overall in the championship to John Surtees on the MV Agusta, as many faster machines also proved more fragile. But by now the Gileras and Nortons were proving superior, and arguably BMW didn't help itself on the track by experimenting with leading link suspension designs, known as Earles forks (after the inventor, Englishman Ernie Earles). Zeller's bike was notoriously difficult to master, in particular because of its quirky handling due almost entirely to the Earles forks, which simply weren't suited to racing.

On the road though the forks were much more effective, as was proven two years after the first race bike appeared with them. Indeed, BMW excelled itself with the 1955 R69 in all respects, as this was a machine acclaimed for its blend of performance and sophistication. It was the first road BMW to feature Earles forks and also came with a revised diaphragm spring clutch as well as various other changes. The 594cc twin produced 35 bhp, as on the R68 enough for 100 mph, but the handling and ride quality were much improved.

In the same year, the R26 made its debut as the first BMW single with Earles forks. Despite its odd trait of rising under braking rather than dipping as telescopic forks do, the ride quality was much improved. This was further helped by the swingarm rear suspension, which had more generous travel than the old plunger type, overall comfort was transformed. 1955 also saw the R51/3 replaced by the R50, which received the same

< These 1955 police R69s were fitted with the large 'dustbin' fairings seen briefly in racing before being banned. Stability in crosswinds was poor so they weren't always popular.

engine and chassis improvements—including the Earles forks—as the R69.

The principle behind Earles forks is identical to the more familiar twin shock and swingarm rear suspension. Horizontal tubes pivot on the steered downtubes with their movement controlled by a pair of shock absorbers. Compared with telescopic forks, the penalty is high steered and unsprung mass (which is why they didn't work as well under racing conditions), but they were more rigid and the scope for increased wheel travel was better. Damping control proved easier too—damping was still very crude on telescopic forks in the 1950s and through most of the 1960s too. After they appeared on the R69, BMW continued to use Earles forks until the end of the 1960s, by which time telescopic forks were sufficiently developed and sophisticated to be superior in comfort, control, and ride quality, as well as in outright high performance. BMW suffered no loss of face in going

> BMW's three-wheeled Isetta bubble car of 1954, an Italian Iso design built under license, was famous for its front-opening door.

back to them as, after all, the Germans had introduced them in the first place!

BMW had lost its Eisenach car factory to East Germany after the war, so it began car production instead in Munich, starting with the luxury 501 to get things moving again. But the real demand was, as in the motorcycle market, for small utility cars, which BMW met with the Isetta bubble car. This generally had a pair of close-set rear wheels with two normally sited ones at the front corners, although in some markets where tax brackets favored three wheelers, a single back wheel was used. This was an Italian design built under license to Iso, and famous for its front-opening door and barely adequate 250cc and 300cc engines.

In 1956 BMW offered a bike for those riders who wanted a softer option than the sporting R69, calling it the R60. This shared the 594cc capacity of the R69, but produced just 28 bhp at 5600 rpm, meaning it struggled to reach 90 mph.

< *The 1956 R60 shared the R69's 594cc capacity but produced just 28 bhp at 5600 rpm. It replaced the R67 and shared the R50/R69 chassis with Earles forks and swingarm rear suspension.*

There was compensation though in increased low rev torque and a gentler power delivery. The R60 was a replacement for the R67, last of the old-type pre-war-derived twins, and shared the R50/R69 chassis complete with Earles forks and swingarm rear suspension.

The 1950s marked the first time BMW decided to target the American market specifically, doing its best to boost sales across the Atlantic with special US versions of many of its machines. The R69 for example came with higher bars, and owners would then customize their bikes further with screens, extra spotlights, panniers and so on. But sales of all the new, big, and expensive twins were low around the world—less than 5,000 of the 600s were sold by the end of the 1950s as people turned to the new generation of cheap, small cars in Europe, and cheap bigger ones in the US!

> BMW offered special US versions of its machines such as this R69, which has also been personalized with contemporary screen, panniers, and spotlights.

1957 *through* 1969

Decline, fall, and a second recovery

In 1956 the prospects were still looking good for BMW, despite the first signs of a slide in sales. The company was producing some of the world's best motorcycles as well as fine sports cars, the Isetta was selling well, and the aero engine division was strong too. In 1948 motorcycle production returned to Munich from Eisenach (where it had run from 1942 to 1944), and it stayed there until moving to Spandau, Berlin, in 1969. But by the end of the 1950s the production lines were slowing, as sales dwindled and worldwide motorcycle markets shrank.

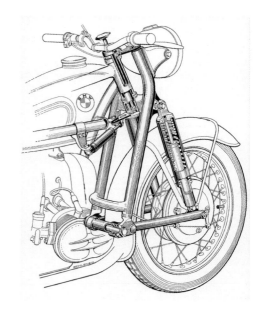

Earles forks were used until the end of the 1960s. The horizontal tubes pivoted on the steered downtubes with their movement being controlled by a pair of shock absorbers.

> The production lines at Munich slowed toward the end of the 1950s as sales dwindled and worldwide motorcycle markets shrank.

By 1959 financial trouble loomed for BMW, along with many other long-established motorcycle manufacturers. BMW's financial situation was so bad a takeover looked inevitable. Relinquishing control to Mercedes was a likely prospect; that could have meant the eventual end of the BMW name, or possibly just to BMW motorcycles, as Mercedes had little interest in them and the market situation was so poor worldwide. But the Mercedes sale fell through after banker Dr. Herbert Quandt offered substantial backing to BMW, sold the aero engine division, and restored

Banker Dr. Herbert Quandt provided substantial backing to BMW in 1959, saving the company and restoring confidence.

> BMW's 1960s revival was helped by large police orders. Here the Munich police are using modified 1960 R50s, painted white and fitted with the usual police accoutrements.

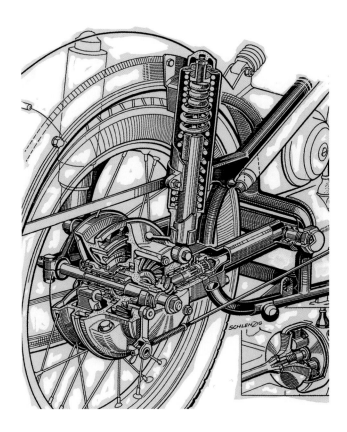

The extended rear loop frame design was retained on BMW's new swingarm, so the twin shock absorbers were each mounted on the back of the loop half way up their bodies, as on this 1960 R27 single.

The shaft final drive and suspension layout of the 1960 R50/2 and all the twins of the time was the same in principle as on the singles. An additional mounting to the mudguard at the top added strength and rigidity. The final drive bevel housing also incorporated the expanding shoe drum brake.

A grid full of BMW outfits open the 1965 grand prix round at the Nürburgring. Eventual champions were the Anglo-Swiss team of Fritz Scheidegger and passenger John Robinson, six points clear of Deubel-Hörner.

business confidence generally. The Quandt family still controls BMW today.

BMW's revival after 1959 was helped by large police orders during the 1960s. Modified R50s were common, painted white and fitted with the usual police accoutrements. The bikes were used for a range of duties, and ironically they proved most versatile in cities becoming increasingly clogged by the very cars that were so damaging to BMW's sales!

By 1960 the rear suspension design was well established and used on both the twins and singles. The twin shock absorbers were each mounted onto an extended rear frame loop half-way up their bodies and, to cope with the additional wheel travel, a proper universal joint replaced the flexible rubber connection used on the old plunger suspension machines. Confirmation that BMW was healthy again came in 1967 when the company produced its 250,000th

< In 1964 Max Deubel and passenger Emil Hörner won their fourth successive world championship, taking victories at Spa and the Isle of Man TT on the way.

machine to be made since World War II, and still the dedication to reliability and quality was undeflected—indeed, it was pulling BMW through.

Although grand prix racing had left BMW behind in the 1960s, the Germans completely dominated sidecar racing, which had far stronger audience appeal then than it does today. By 1964 the highly successful BMW sidecar racers Max Deubel and passenger Emil Hörner had won their fourth successive world championship, and by 1965 a typical starting grid was almost totally filled with BMW-powered outfits. It was a trend that would continue right up to 1974, when two-stroke König engines took over, but until then BMW seemed to have total control. Klaus Enders took the world sidecar championship an astounding six times between 1967 and 1974, partnered by Ralf Engelhardt every year but one, and in the 1973 season their domination was absolute, as they won seven of the eight championship rounds, finishing with a 27-point lead.

Six of the top ten machines in the final championship ratings that year were BMW-powered, and 19 out of 20 possible titles up to 1974 went to BMW.

> *Klaus Enders took the world sidecar championship an astounding six times between 1967 and 1974, partnered by Ralf Engelhardt every year but one. Here in the 1973 season their domination was absolute, as they won seven of the eight championship rounds, finishing with a 27-point lead.*

1969 *through* 1993

A *new generation of twins, fours, triples, and singles*

As far as road bikes were concerned the end of the 1960s was the end of an era for BMW, but much more importantly, the distinct beginning of an exciting new one. The Quandt management had turned the company's fortunes around, enough for a major new investment program to be effected, and which resulted in a raft of dramatic new models being rolled out in 1969. These were the /5 series machines, and they were so different that many BMW traditionalists were upset by them, rather than welcoming the changes— it didn't help that the singles had all been phased out by then! The Earles forks were dropped and the engines were entirely new, with camshafts

> The 1960s ended dramatically with three new models for 1969, including the 498cc R50/5 (here with high-rise US handlebars).

> The biggest new 1969 machine was the 746cc R75/5, sharing the 70.6mm stroke of the R50/5 and R60/5 but with an 82mm bore. Power was 50 bhp at 6500 rpm.

positioned beneath the cranks instead of above as before, while plain instead of roller bearings were used in conjunction with a high pressure oil system. The electrics were a thoroughly modern 12 volts, and electric start was an option. The new frame, like so many of the time (and plenty even today) was closely based on the iconic Norton Featherbed, constructed in tubular steel featuring two main loops cradling the engine. The rear shocks were now mounted top and bottom using the rear subframe, modern-style. And BMW was back with conventional telescopic forks.

Three bikes were introduced in '69: the 498cc R50/5, 599cc R60/5, and the biggest new model, the 746cc R75/5, which shared the 70.6mm stroke of its smaller siblings but with an 82mm bore. Power of the 750 was 50 bhp at 6500 rpm. The bikes came with big price increases over the old 1968 models, so there was certainly an element of risk for BMW, as the combination of dramatic

The 1973 R60/6 featured five gears instead of four and the longer wheelbase of the previous /5 models, as well as a smaller fuel tank and detail changes.

change with substantial price increases could have stifled sales. But there was no doubt (except among BMW's more conservative customers) that big changes were needed in order to keep the company viable against the rapidly advancing Japanese manufacturers. Honda was by now already proving wrong all those who'd said big capacity bikes were beyond the Orientals with its epochal CB750, while the British manufacturers underscored the futility of doing nothing and investing little by going bust one after the other throughout the 1960s. Indeed, by the early 1970s, the UK, once the world's biggest motorcycle producing nation, didn't have a single significant manufacturer left in business.

By contrast, BMW's 1960s decisions to invest and change proved well judged: in 1973, as the last British manufacturer, Triumph, was going through its painful and drawn out death throes, BMW's sales were reasonably strong at around 25,000

The R75/6 was the first production BMW to be fitted with a front disc brake. The standard fuel tank is pictured here but, like the R60/6 and R90/6, a larger tank was an option.

All attention in 1973 was focused on the R90S, another classic BMW. Engine capacity increased to 898cc, thanks to 90mm pistons and the same 70.6mm stroke, with power up to 67 bhp at 7000 rpm, good enough for a top speed of more than 120 mph.

annually. The company maintained its momentum as the /6 models replaced the /5 machines, although the slow-selling R50/5 was dropped from the range. The R60/6 featured five gears instead of four and the longer wheelbase of the last /5 models, as well as a smaller fuel tank and detail changes. Production numbers now seemed small compared with the tens of thousands of machines coming out of Japan, but it demonstrated a truth which was standing well the test of time: there is always a market for premium quality.

The R75/6 arrived at the same time as the R60/6, and for the first time on a production BMW, it used a front disc brake. Like the R60/6 the instruments were modernized, the side panels altered, and other details changed, causing the weight to increase 22 lb to 441 lb, but its historical significance was the front brake.

But most peoples' attention in 1973 was focused on the R90S, one of the all-time classic BMWs. The engine capacity was taken up to 898cc by the fitment of 90mm pistons, making it the first BMW of more than 750cc. As the 70.6mm stroke was left unchanged the bike gained revvy, over-square dimensions. Power increased to 67 bhp at 7000 rpm, good enough for a top speed of more than 120 mph, and setting this sporting BMW right up with the highest performing bikes of the time. It handled well too, and its glamour was enhanced by the twin front disc brakes, a bar-mounted nose fairing, and a very sophisticated smoked-edge paint finish. In 1976, Helmut Dähne won the Isle of Man TT Production race on an R90S, while Steve McLaughlin and Reg Pridmore scored first and second in the Superbikes race at Daytona—the bike lacked the outright power of some of its competition, but it more than compensated with fine handling, light weight, and balance.

It wasn't the only BMW 900 (although you might have thought so at the time): the softer

R90/6 arrived alongside the R90S and in fact proved just as popular. Around 20,000 examples each of both bikes were sold in the next three years. Power of the /6 was 60 bhp at 6500 rpm, and a single front disc was fitted. The engine (aside from the cylinders and heads), along with most of the chassis were common to the entire /6 range and the 90S, lending BMW much better economies of scale than its relatively small production numbers might have suggested.

Three years later this robust motor grew once again, its bore increasing to 94mm for a capacity of 980cc. The new R100 engine was fitted to BMW's first fully-faired machine (and the first on any mass produced bike of the modern era), the outstanding R100RS. As well as looking good, the fairing provided exceptional weather protection and high speed stability. In the same year, the R100S replaced the R90S, although at first it used a 65 bhp version of the new 980cc engine, where

The softer R90/6 proved just as popular as the R90S—around 20,000 examples of each were sold in the next three years. Power was 60 bhp at 6500 rpm, and a single front disc was fitted.

The R100/7 used a 60 bhp version of the 980cc engine, which had a broader spread of torque better to suit touring. Purpose-made touring accessories such as Krauser-designed panniers and a screen were available directly from BMW.

<< In 1976 BMW increased the bore size to 94mm for a capacity of 980cc in its new R100 engine, fitted to its first fully faired machine, the R100RS. It provided exceptional weather protection and high-speed stability.

< The R100S of 1976 replaced the R90S, although at first it used a 65 bhp version of the new 980cc engine, where the R100RS produced 70 bhp. But from 1978 the R100S used the RS motor. The R100 series engine was distinguished externally by new rocker covers with four instead of two horizontal fins and on some models a black finish.

the R100RS produced 70 bhp. But from 1978 the R100S used the RS motor.

But BMW's nod toward performance was looking half-hearted, especially in the face of some very quick Japanese bikes such as Kawasaki's Z1/Z900 series and two-stroke triples; so, BMW kept moving forward at what it was best at: sophistication, quality, and comfort. There was a softer option to the sporting S and RS models in the R100/7: the 980cc engine produced just 60 bhp in this guise but had a broader spread of torque better to suit touring. In a highly unusual move, purpose-made touring accessories such as Krauser-designed panniers and a screen were available directly from BMW—this is widespread practice today but unheard of at the time, when it was considered a major marketing innovation.

In the most fundamental terms, BMW's assault on the 1970s was successful: the company survived the devastating Japanese onslaught that finished off so many other European manufacturers and almost did the same for Harley-Davidson.

BMW had stood aside from the growing horsepower and performance race to cultivate the virtues of the boxer twin. But crucially, the company's other deeply ingrained principles, those aerospace-derived values of sophisticated design and high build quality, were also helping to see it through. The British, European, and American factories were plagued by unreliability issues originating from shoddy manufacturing and cheap-skate design, just as the Japanese were proving to be masters of mass production, ramping up quality standards to entirely new levels. While many other factories also offered bikes with their own unique virtues, customers were put off by their bad execution. Who wants the best handling, best looking, or most individual bike if it keeps letting you down at the side of the road? BMW's twins offered a range of factors not found in Japanese bikes, but with matching or better levels of reliability and quality to justify their premium price. They weren't going to sell in huge numbers, but they were going to sell enough.

Even though the boxer twin's virtues might have been a unique selling point, that configuration shackled BMW as much as singling it out. The motor could never produce the outright power of a four (the configuration which was to dominate the big bike racing classes), and as the 1970s progressed, the attractions of four-cylinder engines being campaigned so effectively by the Japanese appeared to shake BMW's faith in the boxer twin as its sole engine type. The Berlin factory was financially sound once again, forging its own path, and although any power deficit inherent in its unique and defining engine layout was compensated for by light weight and secure handling, the now aging twin was struggling to meet new noise and emissions laws. So plans and investment

The Berlin factory had re-established itself by the late 1970s as a financially sound manufacturer forging its own path. But the twin was aging and plans for an entirely new engine were being made.

The 1976 599cc R60/7 replaced the R60/6, although the changes were relatively few. The switchgear was revised and the seat improved.

The 1976 R75/7 was replaced in 1977 by the R80/7, its capacity increased to 797cc after a bore increase to 84.8mm. Power was 55 bhp at 7000 rpm. Many BMW fans considered this the best capacity for the boxer twin.

funding for an entirely new engine were being laid out even before the end of the 1970s.

Meanwhile, the existing models weren't being neglected, nor were the more prosaic market sectors. While the R100RS grabbed the glamour in 1976, so the 599cc R60/7 replaced the R60/6, although the changes were relatively few. The traditional 750 capacity was offered the same year by the 746cc R75/7, which combined the ubiquitous 70.6mm stroke with an 82mm bore.

The R75/7 lasted only one year though, being superseded in 1977 by the R80/7, its capacity increased to 797cc via a bore increase to 84.8mm. Many BMW fans to this day consider the 800 as the best expression of this generation of boxer twins, for its combination of torque and smoothness, and useful 55 bhp power output at 7000 rpm.

The following year, in 1978, BMW built its smallest ever boxer, the 473cc R45. The bike was aimed at a legally defined German horsepower

In 1978 BMW built its smallest boxer, the 473cc R45. The German market model's 27 bhp was too feeble for its weight—even the 35 bhp foreign market version was considered very slow. The near-identical 649.6cc R65 was more successful.

The basic 1978 R100T shared the RS's 980cc engine producing 70 bhp at 7250 rpm, but at 437 lb it weighed a full 79 lb less and so performed better.

category, but its 27 bhp was simply too feeble for its weight, and even the 35 bhp foreign market version was considered very slow. The R45 was successful only in Germany. Fortunately the near-identical 649.6cc R65 launched alongside it was much more successful, thanks to a successful styling exercise which gave the traditional twin a thoroughly contemporary look, and a much livelier engine.

By 1978 BMW was fully focused on the touring sector, and just as Harley was producing basic custom bikes as a canvas for its customers to begin personalizing their machines, so BMW was doing the same for touring riders. Thus the fully faired and well-equipped 1978 R100RT was complemented by the far more basic R100T, which shared the same 980cc engine producing 70 bhp at 7250 rpm, but which at 437 lb weighed a full 79 lb less (and so performed considerably better), and which was designed for customers to fit their own touring equipment.

BMW surprised everyone though in 1980, not with the fruition of its by-then-widely-leaked plans to build a four-cylinder bike of its own, but ironically by unveiling an unexpected twin. The R80G/S (Gelände/Strasse, or off-road/street) dumbfounded many observers, as nothing like it had been seen before. Technically it was interesting, with highly advanced features such as all-aluminum, ceramic-plated cylinders and single-sided swingarm with monoshock. But the real shock, if you'll excuse the pun, came with what it was supposed to do: despite the huge twin-cylinder engine, this was a trail bike! Most observers simply weren't sure what to make of the G/S, but as it turned out, this was the machine that single-handedly invented the big-capacity trail-bike category. It also established a special BMW feature in this class which has been sustained ever since: it was more than a

The R80G/S (Gelände/Strasse, or off-road/street) was a surprise. The bike single-handedly invented the big capacity trail bike category and featured technical innovations such as all-aluminum, ceramic-plated cylinders and a single-sided swingarm with monoshock.

The R65LS fell between style and tradition while satisfying neither. The 650 twin featured an angular nose fairing with sporty low handlebars and a matt black finish on the exhaust system. Power was 50 bhp at 7250 rpm.

> *The 1982 R100CS replaced the R100S. The 70 bhp engine was unchanged apart from more durable and lighter all-aluminum cylinders and lightweight clutch.*

styling exercise; the bike actually worked remarkably well off-road as well as on it, as proved convincingly in 1981 when Hubert Auriol won the grueling Paris-Dakar rally on a G/S.

The timing couldn't have been better. During the 1980s the motorcycle-as-utility-machine gave way in western markets to the motorcycle-as-leisure-vehicle. BMW's invention of the big trail bike class was almost casual, but it perfectly foretold the new market direction right at its outset: no one needed a big capacity trail bike, but more and more riders really, really wanted one. It was cool.

Not all the company's efforts were as successful though. Alongside the imaginative R80G/S, the effort to spruce up the R65 in 1981 looked uninspired. The new bike, called the R65LS, fell somewhere between style and tradition while satisfying neither camp. It featured an angular nose fairing with sporty low handlebars and a matt black finish to the exhaust system. Power was still 50 bhp at

7250 rpm, which undermined the sporting intentions implied by the style. In 1982 there was a tacit recognition that BMW was now well off the pace of the Japanese in pure performance terms: the R100CS appeared in this year as a replacement for the R100S, although its 70 bhp engine was unchanged apart from using the more durable and lighter all-aluminum cylinders and a lightweight clutch, both seen first on the R80G/S. The CS stood for Classic Sport, confirmation that this was no longer a sports bike in terms that could be measured in lap times or other hard figures, but carried a vaguer definition of attitude which other European manufacturers were also falling back on. This new realm was no less valid in the eyes of many enthusiasts, but it was nevertheless a confirmation that BMW was moving out of the performance mainstream it had once inhabited comfortably two decades and more before.

A bike too prescient for its own good, meanwhile, was the R80ST, also of 1982. This was based on the G/S and included its monoshock, single-sided swingarm and high-rise exhaust, but the suspension and wheels were purely road items. The result was a worthy but unexceptional machine, although its equivalent today would be something between a streetfighter and supermoto, now a fast growing class.

By 1982 anyone interested in the German factory, or indeed motorcycles in general, was treading water, just waiting to see what BMW's new fours would be like. The company's near-obsession with individuality ensured the German four would be like no other. Indeed, come 1983 the new K-series machines arranged their engines in an unprecedented way. The liquid-cooled, fuel-injected double overhead cam K100 engine was BMW's response to the Japanese, the same and yet utterly different, as the cylinders were horizontal and the

< The 1982 R80ST was based on the R80G/S and used its monoshock, single-sided swingarm, and high-rise exhaust. But the suspension and wheels were purely road items.

The liquid-cooled, fuel-injected double-overhead-cam, four-cylinder K100 engine of 1983. The cylinders were horizontal and the crank aligned along the bike to facilitate shaft drive. Old-fashioned 67mm x 70mm long stroke dimensions and overly short conrods were used to minimize width.

The 1983 K100 was a success, suggesting BMW's plan to phase out the twins was on course. The chassis was all-new and incorporated the engine as a stressed frame component.

crank aligned along the bike (just like a boxer twin's), to facilitate shaft drive. It was technically very advanced in many ways, but the design was also compromised, using old-fashioned 67mm x 70mm long stroke dimensions and overly short conrods for compactness. It might seem esoteric, but long conrods are a favorite modification of tuners of all types of engine, as they slow the piston acceleration around the top dead center region, and that improves efficiency and power output. As much for the respect engendered by the badge as its performance, the 1983 K100 was a success, even though early examples suffered reliability problems. But these were corrected, while the high levels of vibration were mostly over-shadowed by excitement at the sheer boldness of the design. The chassis was all-new too, incorporating the engine as a stressed frame component—a relatively new idea that saved weight and improved handling. The design's modularity also lent itself to the production of three-cylinder versions, expanding the potential market at a relatively low additional cost.

Now a BMW aficionado could choose a multi without following the crowd; there would be triples as well as fours and this, combined with the evident popularity of the new K-series (despite those early difficulties), set in motion another plan: to phase out production of the 1000 cc twins altogether!

It all seemed like a good idea at the time. But approaching the 1990s the typical motorcyclist was less the young, penurious refugee car driver of old, but more affluent and educated with time and money to spare. His requirements (and increasingly, her requirements) had little to do with economy and more with hedonism, while the performance of almost all motorcycles, Japanese and European (if not American), began to exceed the riding capabilities of the majority of riders. This

BMW dubbed its engine and transmission design the
Compact Drive System, the five-speed gearbox,
clutch, and shaft drive all being as short as physically
possible to fit within the wheelbase.

The civilian version of the K100RT offered exceptional weather protection; panniers came as standard fitment.

> *In 1984 the sportier K100RS was distinguished by its slim fairing that reached down to the top of the engine. Power was 90 bhp, although the suspension was made firmer to carry the extra weight of the fairing and provide sharper handling.*

meant that attributes such as style, individuality, and character held greater value, traits that are inherent with the boxer twin package. And if the performance of the twins wasn't as good as the fours, for the majority of riders it was plenty good enough. Far from signaling BMW's path to oblivion, this was a turning point in motorcycling history, when the particular appeal of characterful engines such as V-twins, parallel twins, triples, and of course boxer twins, was rising once more, to overcome the power advantage of the dominant fours.

To be candid, BMW hadn't spotted this; it's only clear in retrospect. So briefly (a duration of months, not years), BMW missed the new direction in which the markets were headed and, in 1986, stopped production altogether of the big boxer twins. The production of 450cc and 800cc boxers did not stop at this time.

The base 1984 R80 featured the swingarm and clutch from the R80G/S with detail internal changes which made it much smoother. Power was down 2 bhp to 48 bhp due to emissions regulations.

> The 1985 K75C was the debut triple and shared more than half its components with the K100. Revised cylinder heads meant more power per liter than the fours—75 bhp at 8500 rpm.

The resulting outcry from enthusiasts world-wide brought BMW to its senses, and in a remark-ably short time, production was restarted and the old bikes were revamped while, concurrent with the K-series, an entirely new generation of twins was planned in order to fill this need for soul in a motorcycle. A two- or three-cylinder engine seemed able to deliver it, where a four could only look on from the sidelines.

The model structure for the K-series mean-while was following the same pattern as for the twins. The K100RT of 1984, for example, was the fully faired touring version, in the same mold as the R100RT. As with the twins, the K models proved popular with many police forces, who were particularly attracted by the substantial power advantage over the boxer motors, as the four pro-duced a much stronger 90 bhp at 8000 rpm. The fairing offered exceptional weather protection and panniers now came as standard fitment. The engine's low rev torque particularly suited this role, although high rev vibration was well above average and gear shifting was characteristically clunky and slow.

Arriving also in 1984 was the sportier K100RS, distinguished by a slim fairing that reached down to the top of the engine. The power output was unchanged at 90 bhp, but the suspension was firmer, to deal with the extra weight of the fairing and for sharper handling. More than half of BMW's production already was of K-series machines.

The modularity of the K-series engine allowed BMW in 1985 to introduce its first-ever triple, the 750cc base model K75C. This shared more than half its components with the K100, substantially reducing production costs, while cylinder head modifications released more power per liter than the fours—75 bhp at 8500 rpm came to 100 bhp per liter, the highest specific power output to

date for a production BMW, even though the cam timing and valve sizes were unchanged from the fours. A year later the K75S followed with its small frame-mounted fairing, firmer suspension, and a disc instead of drum rear brake. Although the engine was identical to the K75C, top speed was up 6 mph to 130 mph due to the improved aerodynamics. The three-cylinder bikes were preferred by many riders for their sharper handling due to the reduced weight, and the less busy feel of the engines won fans to the smaller capacity K-series too—a further indication of the growing importance of character.

The extra power of the fours over the twins and triples was put to good use when BMW followed the trend for increased luxury and specification on touring bikes by introducing the K100LT in 1987. The bike featured a massive and highly protective fairing as well as panniers, top box, and even wiring for the fitment of a radio. The rear

< In 1986 the K75S arrived with a small frame-mounted fairing, firmer suspension, and a disc instead of drum rear brake. Speed was up 6 mph to 130 mph due to improved aerodynamics.

The 1987 K100LT featured a large and protective fairing as well as panniers, top box, and even wiring for the fitment of a radio. The rear suspension was self-leveling.

> In fall 1987 the R80GS gained Paralever suspension and was joined by the 980cc R100GS.

suspension was a self-leveling system designed to compensate for the heavy loads it would undoubtedly carry, another innovation for the Germans.

Meanwhile, with interest in the twins revitalized, the new R80GS (the / was dropped by then) appeared as the first platform for BMW's new Paralever rear suspension. This featured a trapezoid geometry between the shaft housing and a torque arm beneath it which altered the response of the rear suspension to changing power loads. Shaft-driven motorcycles were known for excessive vertical reactions to throttle movement, rising at the rear under load and dropping suddenly as the throttle was closed. Paralever was designed to counter this and mimic more closely the behavior of chain driven bikes. The design meant two universal joints were then incorporated into the drive shaft assembly, improving drive smoothness too.

The process of reintroducing the boxer engine continued with some vigor now, as in the fall of

'87 BMW added the 980cc R100GS to its range. The twins were not only back, the one liter twins were back too, despite the now well established one liter fours in the line-up. In the background, work had started on an entirely new range of boxer twins, the first new rather than upgraded models since those /5 series bikes of 1969; they were certainly long overdue. But innovation was continuing in other areas as BMW became the world's first manufacturer to introduce anti-lock braking, or ABS, on production motorcycles. This made its debut, as an optional extra at first, on the K-series bikes in 1988. Via sensors on each wheel a central computer could detect if a wheel's rate of deceleration exceeded prede-termined figures. If it did, the brake pressure would be released briefly then reapplied to prevent lock-up, and the process repeated at around seven times per second. It was relatively crude by today's standards but still very effective and, despite the extra cost, it was taken up by many new BMW buyers.

< *BMW introduced electronic ABS anti-lock brakes on the K-series bikes in 1988, a motorcycling first.*

The boxers' reinstatement kept up its pace with the reappearance of a real old stager, the R80RT which proved especially popular with police forces around the world, along with the military and other large organizations for whom its ease of maintenance and reliability took priority. Changes to the police bikes from civilian versions were relatively few, and included a more powerful alternator, as well as a single seat unit, and additional wiring for lights and radio equipment.

In 1989 BMW introduced the first 16-valve version of the K100 engine in the controversially styled K1. The change to two inlet and two exhaust valves per cylinder and an increase in compression ratio boosted power to 99 bhp, a ceiling voluntarily adhered to in the German market in the face of concerns about the growing power outputs of motorcycles, and one which was carried over by default to export markets too.

It was not its power but the K1's aerodynamic, bulbous styling that caused a stir though, especially as it was subjected to some of the most garish color schemes ever seen on a motorcycle—even the aluminum casings were brightly colored. The bike was optimistically billed by BMW as a supersports machine, a sign perhaps that the company still hankered after a presence in the performance market sector. But compared with the yardstick Yamaha FZR1000 EXUP it was heavy and underpowered, and the Germans surely knew that. As a GT touring bike however the K1 worked much better, and it did well in many countries: the 100,000th K-series was a K1. A year later the 16-valve engine found a second home in the K100RS, boosting power by a now much-needed 10 bhp to 99 bhp at 8000 rpm. The upgraded RS also benefited from the K1's Paralever rear suspension and importantly, its four-piston Brembo front brakes.

The 16-valve 1989 K1 engine featured two inlet and two exhaust valves per cylinder and an increased compression ratio which raised power to 99 bhp.

< The R80RT was a reintroduced old-type boxer. Changes to the police bikes were relatively few, and included a more powerful alternator as well as single seat unit and additional wiring for lights and radio equipment.

The K1's aerodynamic but bulbous styling caused a
stir in 1989, especially as some garish color schemes
were used. The 100,000th K-series was a K1.

The K1's 16-valve engine was fitted to the K100RS in 1990, boosting power by 10 bhp to 99 bhp at 8000 rpm, with more torque. The bike also benefited from the K1's four-piston Brembo front brakes.

By this time the majority of K-series bikes also came with ABS.

Development appeared to be moving slowly and steadily at BMW in the early 1990s, which is also when the company made its one millionth motorcycle. The company firmly rejected the performance race being fought so furiously in the sports bike markets. Existing models were being upgraded, refined, and improved in entirely predictable ways; the twins were selling well again alongside the triples and fours; and a reasonably successful if quiet existence was assured, satisfying mature riders who valued fuel range, touring comfort, high residual values, and longevity ahead of the quickest lap times and fashion-led styling changes. The nearest we got to radical change came with the first capacity increase for the K-series in 1992. The touring K1100LT's 1092cc capacity was achieved by a bore increase to

70.5mm. Power remained at 99 bhp, albeit at a slightly low 7500 rpm, but torque increased to 79 lb-ft at 5500 rpm, against the K100RS's 74 lb-ft at 6750 rpm.

> *The first capacity increase for the K-series came in 1992 with the touring K1100LT, its 1092cc achieved by a bore increase to 70.5mm. Power was 99 bhp at 7500 rpm, torque was 79 lb-ft at 5500 rpm.*

1993 *to* present

The renaissance

Behind the scenes, radical things were happening, and in 1993 the world was shown the results. After being reminded of the true value of the boxer engine in 1986, BMW had been working furiously behind the scenes to produce an entirely new one. The R1100RS unveiled in '93 was the result, and in true BMW fashion, the new bikes were new to an almost extreme sense. The R259 engine, as it was designated, was still recognizably a BMW air-cooled boxer twin, but now the camshafts were sited high in the cylinder heads alongside the valves, driven by chain from an auxiliary shaft underneath the crankshaft—this near-overhead cam design (called high cam) helped performance

The all-new R1100RS of 1993 had an eight-valve, air-cooled, fuel-injected 1085cc boxer engine designated the R259. Twin 'high' cams were sited alongside the valves, driven by chain from an auxiliary shaft below the crank, to minimize engine width.

without increasing engine width. The 1085cc motor was fuel-injected, powerful, and smooth, yet ironically the bike's chassis was even more radical. Indeed, the engine was the chassis: the rear Paralever suspension and drive shaft were bolted to the back, while an all-new suspension design called Telelever was bolted to the front. There was no frame at all, just a subframe for the seat and steering assembly.

Telelever is composed of telescopic legs clamped in a single, pivoting upper yoke and located just above the mudguard by a wishbone which pivots on the engine. Dive under braking is reduced by 90 percent, although unsprung weight compared with conventional telescopic forks is increased. BMW had introduced telescopic forks in 1935, moved on to Earles forks when they were superior, returned to teles again in 1969, and now the Germans were forging their own path yet again. BMW devotees immediately insisted

BMW Grafik Design VT-T

In 1990 BMW began work on the prototypes for a radical new front suspension system called Telelever. This comprised telescopic legs clamped in a single, pivoting upper yoke and located just above the mudguard by a wishbone.

The F650 of 1993 used a liquid-cooled 652cc single-cylinder engine designed in conjunction with Rotax and Aprilia. It was the first BMW ever to feature chain drive.

Telelever was superior, others saw it as merely being different for its own sake, which undoubtedly was a factor with BMW. The reality fell somewhere between: most engineering solutions are a balance between advantages and compromise; Telelever simply offered a different set of advantages and compromises to telescopic forks. For riders who value the advantages, they're better, for others the case is less clear. But one thing not in doubt is that BMW was true to its nature!

BMW pushed its own boundaries forward in other ways that year. The F650 showed how the ability to think out of the box extended beyond pure engineering: although the new liquid-cooled 652cc single-cylinder trail bike was conventional in contemporary terms, it was still the first BMW to feature chain final drive, and also the first to be produced outside of Germany. It was designed in cooperation with Austrian engine specialist Rotax and rising Italian company Aprilia. Production was

The F650 was the first BMW produced outside Germany, made by Aprilia at its Noale factory.

contracted out to Aprilia, which ran a line dedicated to the F650 at its factory in Noale near Venice. The bike was developed alongside Aprilia's Pegaso, although detail differences meant few components were interchangeable—the Aprilia engine for example featured a five-valve cylinder head compared with BMW's four valves. The purists of course didn't like the F650, even though a knowledge of BMW's history should have prepared them for something like this. But, the bike was very successful anyway, continuing in production and selling well today. Indeed, if there's one lesson BMW purists should learn from the company's history, it's that they've always been proved wrong when they resist something new! The arrival of the F650 also meant that in the early 1990s, BMW was the only manufacturer in the world to offer one-, two-, three-, and four-cylinder engines in its range.

The R100RT of 1995 was dubbed the Classic in deference to this being the final year of the old engine.

< The 1994 R100R Mystik, a special version of the 1992 R100R, was the last model with the old engine to be made when production ceased at the end of 1995.

Despite the arrival of the new twin, the old-type boxers were still in demand. A year after the R1100RS was introduced BMW brought out the R100R Mystik, a special version of the 1992 R100R, which had been BMW's best-selling model. The 60bhp 980cc engine had distinctive rounded valve covers and various cosmetic adornments, and the Mystik became the last model to be introduced with the old engine. Production ceased at the end of 1995. The R100RT was being offered alongside, and in 1995 this was enhanced and called the Classic, in deference to this being the end of the line for the old engine. It was available into 1996 as stocks ran out.

Production of the old motors ceased altogether in 1996, the very last machine being an R80GS Basic which rolled off the Berlin line on December 19, 1996. As the bikes with the old engines were phased out, so new eight-valve versions took their place. For example, the R1100RT

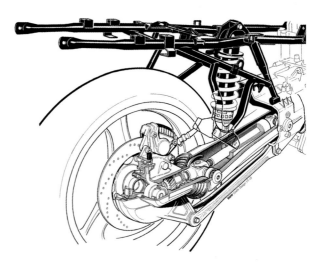

The Paralever system was introduced in 1987 on the R80GS, then modified for the new R1100RS boxer (pictured) in 1993. Two universal joints were incorporated in the drive shaft.

< In 1996 the R1100RT arrived as the flagship touring twin. The engine and transmission were identical to those of the R1100RS apart from an altered final drive ratio, and Telelever and Paralever suspension were used.

In 1999, the GS series enjoyed another upgrade when the R1150GS replaced the R1100GS. Despite its off-road attire, the GS owes much of its popularity to touring riders.

took over as the flagship touring twin in 1996, with an engine and transmission identical to those of the R1100RS, except for an altered final drive ratio. Telelever and Paralever suspension were fitted. The upper fairing was revised for sleeker looks in 2001.

The year 1993 was important for another reason: it was when American David Robb was installed as head of motorcycle design. Robb asked a simple question: why did BMW produce only touring bikes? There was no convincing answer, so Robb instigated a change of thinking that was to transform the company's fortunes and project it into the most successful period in its long history, by a large margin. But it depended on the success of a single bike, the K1200RS slated for launch in 1997, and as it turned out, it was touch and go.

Meanwhile, the S suffix—made legendary on the R90S a quarter of a century earlier—made a comeback on the R1100S at the end of 1998, by

In 1997 the K1200RS grew to 1171cc and output leaped to 128 bhp. The dramatic styling came from changes in attitude precipitated by design chief David Robb.

The R1200C of 1997 and its 850cc sibling, the R850C of 1999, proved BMW could produce a custom bike and tap into a lucrative new sector yet remain original and true to its principles.

which time some 140,000 new-generation boxers had been built in Berlin. This was the most powerful boxer yet, producing 98 bhp at 7500 rpm, and it featured BMW's first six-speed gearbox plus improved Telelever with reduced unsprung weight. Top speed was 142 mph, still no match for the Japanese, or indeed Ducati or Aprilia twin-cylinder superbikes, but it was enough for many riders, and the handling was exceptionally stable.

The ever-popular GS series was treated to the new motor, then in 1999 it was uprated yet again when the R1150GS took over from the R1100GS. The 1130cc engine had a bore and stroke of 101mm x 73mm, making it the biggest capacity trail bike ever produced by any manufacturer. But its popularity continued to grow, and it was one of BMW's best selling models, appealing mostly to touring riders despite the off-road style.

Robb's thinking looked far beyond a mild upgrade of an existing model though. In 1997 the

The 1171cc K-series engine was used in 1999 to power the luxury tourer K1200LT. Features included electric reverse drive, integrated sound system, electrically adjustable screen and optional heated seats.

The S suffix made a comeback on the R1100S at the end of 1998. It was the most powerful boxer yet, producing 98 bhp at 7500 rpm, and featured BMW's first six-speed gearbox. Top speed was 142 mph.

company released the new K1200RS, a bike he describes as the most important of his tenure. The four-cylinder engine had grown to 1171cc, but output had leaped to 128 bhp, smashing the politically motivated 100 bhp limit (except in countries where it was a legal requirement, of course). Yet the significance of the bike went far beyond this: the styling was absolutely dramatic and utterly different, nothing like anything BMW had done or indeed anyone else. And if the bike had failed, Robb's ideas would have been deemed to have gone the same way and the raft of subsequent bold new models pivotal to BMW's future direction would not have happened. Some markets, notably the UK (one of BMW's bigger export markets), disliked the bike, but overall it did well. Just well enough for Robb to be given the green light to continue his mission. Sure enough, later the same year, BMW did the unthinkable and brought out a bike which was pitched into the lucrative

In 2001, the R1150R replaced the R1100R and showed that even a conventional, unfaired BMW boxer could be a stunningly attractive machine.

The C1, BMW's first scooter, first two-stroke and, at 124cc, its smallest engine. The roof is an integral part of the C1's passive safety system.

cruiser sector. Yet the new R1200C confirmed this was the right move, the company didn't have to produce only touring bikes to stay true to its philosophy—even a cruiser could be unmistakably a BMW, both visually and in its basic principles. Where almost every other manufacturer had produced its own safe but unimaginative interpretation of the Harley-Davidson V-twin theme, BMW instead produced an effective custom boxer twin with Telelever and Paralever suspension!

Touring bikes weren't forgotten though, and in 1999 the K1200LT was introduced, a full-on luxury touring bike designed to compete with Honda's Gold Wing. The BMW difference was that, unlike the Honda and indeed Harley-Davidson's Electra Glide Ultra Classic, the LT dispensed with the kitsch, glitzy 1960s styling of those two and produced a thoroughly modern look—the company drew parallels with its own 7-Series car.

At the other end of the spectrum, 1999 was the first year of the Boxer Cup, a one-make series for the R1100S which proved highly effective at raising BMW's profile among sport riders who'd never taken much notice of the German bikes before. This quickly became an established part of the racing calendar, earning UEM and FIM status in 2002 and offering highly entertaining support races at a wide range of major events.

In 2000, production of the F650 was brought back to the Spandau, Berlin, factory from Aprilia, now the expansion program there had been completed. The range of new models was proving more popular than even the most optimistic forecasts might have predicted, and production that year exceeded 70,000 units, almost twice previous production highs in the early 1990s and double the earlier peak of 31,515 in 1977. The trend was still strongly upward.

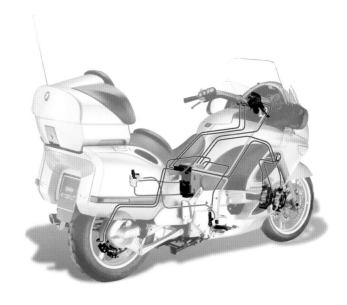

Another innovation introduced in 2001 was Integrated ABS. With this clever electro-hydraulic system, each brake lever operates both front and rear brakes together in a load-sharing arrangement that adapts to varying loads and road conditions.

The most off-road biased of the singles is the F650 GS Dakar, with extra-long-travel suspension. This was thoroughly revised in 2004.

BMW was on a roll now. In 2001 it showed that even a base model motorcycle—the new R1150R—could be stunningly attractive to look at as well as great fun to ride. Not everything was working as well as hoped, however. In 2000 BMW had ventured into a class at least as improbable for the Germans as cruisers: the scooter market. In typical BMW fashion, the new C1 was completely different to anything else and utterly innovative—it was the first scooter or indeed two-wheeler of any type to offer meaningful passive crash protection. It came with a roof as part of a protective cage around the rider, who needed no helmet but who instead was protected by seat belts. The C1 used BMW's smallest ever engine at 124cc. But by 2001 it was clear that the aim of attracting people to scooters who'd previously avoided them because of safety fears wasn't working as well as predicted. Despite a 200cc version appearing in 2001, production was wound down soon after.

The first bike to benefit from BMW's new mission to shed weight was
the R1200GS, thoroughly revised and restyled too. It was an amazing
66 lb lighter than the 1150GS it replaced, and peak power was up 16
bhp to 100 bhp at 7000 rpm.

BMW's reputation wasn't harmed, as the project served to underscore the company's appetite for innovation and lateral thinking. Indeed, 2001 was the same year BMW introduced its Integrated ABS system, which cleverly combined anti-lock brakes with servo-assistance for the first time on a production motorcycle. Each brake lever operates both front and rear brakes together, the rider's effort being enhanced by an ingenious adaptation of the ABS hydraulic pressure pump. The system even adapts to varying loads and road conditions.

This too wasn't popular with all riders—to some it smacked of technology for its own sake rather than to address a real problem (lever effort isn't generally considered an issue on other bikes), but it does show how BMW is constantly pushing into new areas and trying out new ideas. To be bold, innovative, daring, and original, inevitably you will suffer some failures, some neutrals. The

> *BMW entered the touring cruiser sector in 2003 with the R1200CL, in which the 1179cc boxer twin was detuned to a very low 61 bhp at 5000 rpm.*

challenge is to have more successes, which BMW was clearly doing.

New ideas, and a growing wave of new models have taken BMW at a breathtaking pace into the new century. So quickly has it evolved that BMW's model range is now the youngest overall it's ever been, as well as by far its broadest. 2002 saw the arrival of the F650CS, a belt-driven version of the well-established single with radically different styling and a fascinating new on-board storage solution, aimed at entry level riders.

Criticism had been growing however that a value once considered integral to BMW, and especially its boxer twins, was being overlooked: weight. As the Japanese were pouring technology and research into reducing the mass of their bikes, the Germans appeared to be neglecting this area, and BMWs were looking increasingly heavy in comparison. Maybe BMW's eye had been off the ball for a while, but this was now being taken very

< BMW finally returned to the high performance battlefront with the K1200S, its transverse four-cylinder engine producing 165 bhp. The bike also debuted BMW's new Duolever front suspension system.

seriously behind the scenes, and the fruits were unveiled in 2004 with the R1200GS. The bike took the older R1150GS's unique, head-turning chunky style and moved that forward, and in the process also shed an amazing 66 lb. With the extra torque and power gained through increasing the engine size the performance hike was considerable, and sales of the world's favorite adventure tourer shot upward again.

The previous year BMW also introduced the R1200CL, an American-style touring cruiser, and the K1200GT, a high-speed sport tourer more in the European mold. The company was introducing at least two new models a year, and what we didn't know was that many more were being prepared in the secret design studios. Maybe this is why BMW over-reached itself momentarily: in 2004 BMW presented to the world's motorcycle press a bike which looked set to finally pitch it right back into the high performance fray, after

> *If BMW matched the opposition with the K1200S, it trounced them with the K1200R, by far the most powerful unfaired bike on sale at 161 bhp at 10,250 rpm. The R was closely based on the 1200S.*

many decades' absence. The K1200S was conventional in some respects, featuring the same basic transverse four-cylinder engine layout the Japanese had made their own—the limitations of the old K-series layout were just too much to overcome when outright horsepower was the goal. But so much else about the bike was unique or typically BMW: at the rear, power transfer was still via shaft and Paralever, while the front featured yet another entirely new suspension system. Called Duolever, it comprised a double-wishbone arrangement invented by Englishman Norman Hossack in the 1980s, and promised a less harsh ride quality than Telelever but with the same anti-dive properties while braking.

The problem was, the bike just wasn't ready when the press rode it in the summer of 2004. Interestingly, the huge power of that blue and white roundel was evident in many test reports, as a lot of experienced journalists simply assumed the

< BMW's weight reduction program showed impressive results in the revamped 2005 R1200RT, which was some 44 lb lighter than its predecessor, with sharper handling and improved performance as a result.

bike would be alright when it reached the show-rooms—because it was a BMW—and glossed over the problems, including erratic fueling and vague high speed stability. Others highlighted what BMW clearly now knew, that more work needed to be done, and the bike's showroom launch was postponed from September 2004 until spring of the following year, by which time the problems had been addressed.

It was a costly move but BMW bit the bullet to ensure its standards were maintained. When the 165 bhp K1200S did finally arrive, it proved to be a very effective and fabulously fast sport tourer, with an emphasis on sport, which no longer looked misplaced (although to call it supersport would have been misguided). Soon afterward followed the most powerful unfaired bike produced by any company: the K1200R, a brutal-looking beast of a machine, almost as powerful at 161 bhp as the K1200S. BMW's image as staid

> *The ST badge was revived in 2005 for the R1200ST, the bike whose mission was to replace the now aging R1150RS. The upright twin headlamp polarized opinion about the bike's styling.*

manufacturer of sensible touring bikes was now looking ludicrously out of place. The company did indeed make touring bikes—the 2005 R1200RT was a brilliant example, combining outstanding agility (helped by a 44 lb weight loss over its predecessor) with class-leading comfort and weather protection. It boasted the usual array of intelligent BMW details too, and as an option, electrically adjustable suspension which could be altered at the push of a button according to load and riding conditions—another motorcycling first from BMW. The results of BMW's fundamental re-evaluation of the direction it was taking in the early 1990s was now bearing fruit in two ways, each surely beyond even the company's own expectations. By 2005, BMW was a force in a whole array of market sectors, at the same time as it reinforced its dominance as the master of touring bikes. As a way of ensuring its future in an increasingly diverse market, this was the perfect solution. The

< Two of the new models promised for 2006 include the parallel twin-cylinder F800S and F800ST, middleweight machines with belt final drive designed to bridge the gap between BMW's entry level singles and its bigger twins and fours.

second consequence was rather simpler and more obvious: BMW was now selling thousands more motorcycles, more than 90,000 annually, way in excess of anything it had done in the past.

Yet for 2006 the new model development pace has grown hotter than ever, with five machines (at least) due to be released, including an entirely new range of 800cc parallel twins. The new F800 and F800S feature belt final drive, conventional telescopic forks and liquid-cooled, fuel-injected engines, and are designed to bridge the gap in BMW's range between the entry level F650 singles and the big boxer twins and K-series fours. The S suffix lives on with an all-new R1200S replacing the old 1100—more weight loss is promised! The R1200GS is supplemented by a new R1200GS Adventure, with serious long distance credentials and enhanced off-road ability, while the massively powerful K1200S motor has found a third home in the 2006 K1200GT touring bike.

As Helmut Werner Bönsch, former director of BMW's Motorcycle Division, said of Max Friz: "You will quickly find an astounding similarity with the development of organic life: In both cases we see a process of long-term evolution and then, all of a sudden, a rapid mutation, a quantum leap in development."

Quite what that next leap will be only BMW's engineers know now, but as confirmed by this rash of new models, ideas, and themes, the only thing you can expect is that it will be unexpected.

> *The new K-series four-cylinder motor finds another home in 2006 in the K1200GT sports tourer. Power is reduced to 152 bhp to allow an increase in the spread of torque.*

interview

with David Robb,

head of BMW's Motorcycle Design Studio

*(A version of this interview appeared in BMW Rider,
the UK's BMW customer magazine)*

*Responsibility for the rapid and sustained growth of BMW's
motorcycle division in the last decade inevitably lies with a lot
of people. But the more closely you look, the more you keep
coming round to design chief David Robb. Certainly he's in a
position of considerable influence, not just as the man behind
the styling of individual machines, but as the director of a team
of some 25 designers and engineers at BMW's FIZ design studio
in Munich. It'd be nice to think it's called FIZ because the place
is bubbling with ideas, but the name actually comes from
'Forschungs und Innovationszentrum'—Research and Innovation Center. It's just coincidence that it sounds cool!*

Robb moved to head the motorcycle design team in 1993, and he immediately asked some fundamental questions—obvious ones maybe, but at the same time, difficult. "I wanted to know why BMW was only making touring bikes," he says. "We had 19 models covering just two and a half market segments, and we were fighting ourselves for these sectors."

Clearly he was right, but doing something about it was much harder. "We moved to differentiate the RS from the LT, and now you can clearly see what an RS, an LT, or a cruiser is. It used to be hard to tell our models apart." This short statement covers a great deal of anxiety. The 1997 K1200RS was considered a radical move for BMW at the time—its avante garde styling, un-BMW-like attitude and the fact it broke through the company's self-imposed 100 bhp power ceiling by some 30 bhp were all highly experimental from a marketing point of view, and it wasn't especially well received in every one of BMW's markets. But other countries loved it, enough for the possibilities of Robb's vision to be seen, and he was given the go ahead to continue his radical revisions.

Even so, it's sobering to think that had the K1200RS not been a success, it is quite conceivable that BMW's motorcycle division would have drawn in its horns and continued to play safe, which in turn would have meant the whole raft of exciting and original designs we have seen in the nine years since would not have happened. In turn, BMW's extraordinary growth after the K1200RS, which has led the company to its record-breaking 90,000-plus annual output of today, almost certainly would not have happened either. On the quiet then, the K1200RS was absolutely pivotal to the German company's fortunes at the end of the 20th century, and arguably, because of the way in which it vindicated Robb and unleashed him, it's the most influential BMW since the original R32 of 1923, the bike that started it all.

Yet BMW's recent bikes have done more than boost sales, according to Robb: "The industry as a whole has been attracting older people, but the average age of a BMW buyer now is 38, when it was in the mid-40's. And 80 percent of F650 Funduro sales have been to first-time BMW buyers." So the image of the company is being successfully changed to appeal to younger customers—it's expanding down the age scale, which is surely the healthiest way to move forward.

But does Robb worry about upsetting traditionalists with his sometimes challenging designs? "Our tradition is not a 'shape of the fender' kind, but really it's innovation itself. I don't mean only in horsepower terms, and in fact a lot of sport bike technology is incremental rather than innovative.

"BMW has a history of real innovation—we were the first (in the modern era) with a full fairing on the R100RS, there's our Telelever suspension, Paralever, and so on.

> *The last of the 1085cc versions of the R259 engine still in production was the R1100S, the bike which in 1999 revived the famous S suffix. For 2006 this is replaced by the new R1200S—just as the 1100S was the most powerful twin to date when it was introduced, so the 1200S reclaims the title with its 122bhp. It is much lighter than the old model, like most recent BMWs.*

That's not to say we don't refine things too. I'm convinced of the engineering advantages of Telelever for example and we will continue to develop it in all sorts of different ways."

So BMW is appealing to more young customers, but how is the market changing generally? "Ten years ago BMWs were known for their good engineering, reliability, and so on. But people now are buying their bikes for excitement and image. So we have added sex appeal and have spent a lot of time creating things that look better and better as you get closer to them.

"A bike has to be something you're attracted to. You're out in the environment on a bike, whereas you're encapsulated from it in a car.

"In the future things will get even more exciting as we start to 'build lightness in' as Colin Chapman (founder of Lotus Cars) put it. But we see passive safety as an area BMW can be very strong in. Already ABS is very important, with 98 percent of our customers taking it up. We have looked at airbags, but this is very difficult because they have to be motorcycle specific, so they're expensive and time consuming to develop."

How will new BMWs still look like BMWs? Even aside from the highly distinctive boxer twin engine, at the moment BMWs are instantly recognizable. What's the secret of this? "There isn't one formula that fits all categories. A

> At 435 lb, the HP2 is BMW's lightest and most agile boxer. Based on the R1200GS, it has been tailored to the needs of ambitious enduro riders.

GS has an angular, tough look, but an LT is curvy, so the GS 'form vocabulary' wouldn't fit the LT and vice versa."

But they both still look like BMWs! "This has to do with the composition, for example with the engine exposed below and the bodywork above. Any lower body parts are generally silver so they still have a technical look to maintain the composition. There is also an S-shaped line integrated in the shape of BMWs.

"Shapes shouldn't contradict each other—for example, a sharp-edged badge clashes with an elegant shape."

What are the big challenges still facing BMW? "Ergonomics. This is a huge challenge on a motorcycle. If you have bars that can move forward and back, they hit the tank when you turn them. Low footrests compromise ground clearance. You have to take this into account from the beginning, starting with a small bike to accommodate shorter riders, then move the bars, raise the seat, and so on for taller ones."

Will BMW continue to look at new market sectors? "We're not really looking at the moment as we have plenty of bikes just as we are. But there IS some really exciting stuff on the way!"

He's not telling us what it is. And if BMW's past form is anything to go by, few of us would be likely to guess either!

> *The 2006 Adventure version of the R1200GS features a range of off-road-biased modifications, including long-travel suspension and a larger fuel tank.*

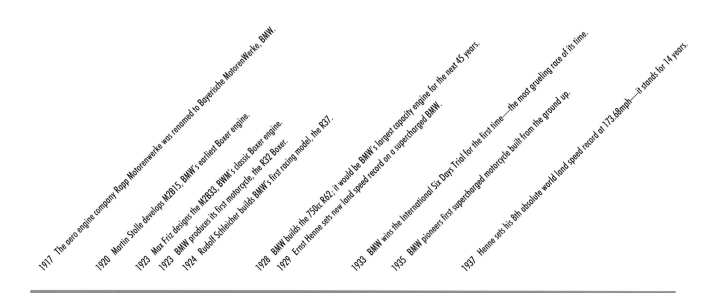

1917 The aero engine company Rapp Motorenwerke was renamed to Bayerische MotorenWerke, BMW.

1920 Martin Stolle develops M2B15, BMW's earliest Boxer engine.

1923 Max Friz designs the M2B33, BWM's classic Boxer engine.

1923 BMW produces its first motorcycle, the R32 Boxer.

1924 Rudolf Schleicher builds BMW's first racing model, the R37.

1928 BMW builds the 750cc R62; it would be BMW's largest capacity engine for the next 45 years.

1929 Ernst Henne sets new land speed record on a supercharged BMW.

1933 BMW wins the International Six Days Trial for the first time—the most grueling race of its time.

1935 BMW pioneers first supercharged motorcycle built from the ground up.

1937 Henne sets his 8th absolute world land speed record at 173.68mph—it stands for 14 years.

1939 Georg Meier becomes the first foreigner on a foreign motorcycle to win Senior TT at the Isle of Man.

1952 BMW produces its first "100mph racer," the R68.

1954 BMW begins a winning streak in sidecar racing, taking the title in 19 of the next 20 years.

1960 BMW's fastest motorcycle yet, the R69S, hits the tarmac.

1973 BMW R75/5 earns Maudes Trophy for performance engineering.

1973 Germany's "Sexiest Superbike," the BMW R90S, is the company's first model to exceed 750cc capacity.

1976 Steve McLaughlin and Reg Pridmore finish 1–2 at Daytona Superbike Competition on R90S.

1976 Lightning-fast R100RS becomes first motorcycle equipped with a full integral fairing.

1980 BMW launches the R80/GS, the first true on-road/off-road machine capable of long distance riding.

1981 Hubert Auriol wins the grueling Paris-Dakar Rally on a BMW R80G/S.

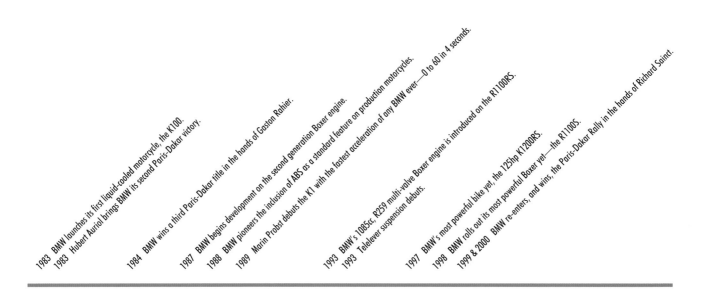

1983 BMW launches its first liquid-cooled motorcycle, the K100.

1983 Hubert Auriol brings BMW its second Paris-Dakar victory.

1984 BMW wins a third Paris-Dakar title in the hands of Gaston Rahier.

1987 BMW begins development on the second generation Boxer engine.

1988 BMW pioneers the inclusion of ABS as a standard feature on production motorcycles.

1989 Marin Probst debuts the K1 with the fastest acceleration of any BMW ever—0 to 60 in 4 seconds.

1993 BMW's 1085cc, R259 multi-valve Boxer engine is introduced on the R1100RS.

1993 Telelever suspension debuts.

1997 BMW's most powerful bike yet, the 125hp K1200RS.

1998 BMW rolls out its most powerful Boxer yet—the R1100S.

1999 & 2000 BMW re-enters, and wins, the Paris-Dakar Rally in the hands of Richard Sainct.

1999 Inaugural running of the **BMW** Motorrad Boxer Cup.

1999 Richard Saint wins the Paris-Dakar-Cairo Rally on a **BMW** F650RR.

2000 **BMW** sweeps the first four positions in the Paris-Dakar Rally.

2002 The **BMW** Motorrad Boxer Cup earns UEM and FIM status.

2003 **BMW** Motorrad celebrates its 80th Anniversary.

2004 **BMW** R1200GS named **Cycle World**'s "Best Open-Class Street Bike" and **Motorcyclist**'s "Motorcycle of the Year."

2004 **BMW**'s fastest motorcycle yet, the K1200S, is released.

2005 **BMW** redefines naked bike performance with the 161hp K1200R.

2005 **BMW** HP2 Enduro is top American finisher at the Baja 1000.

2005 **BMW** K1200R named **Motorcyclist**'s "Motorcycle of the Year."

about the author

English-born Kevin Ash has long been established as one of the best known motorcycle journalists in the UK, as the motorcycle correspondent for The Daily Telegraph newspaper, a prolific writer for most of the British specialist motorcycle press, and weekly columnist for the best selling *Motor Cycle News*. He is also well known internationally as a writer for many foreign publications, including U.S. magazine *Rider,* reporting from new model press introductions around the world and supplying a range of motorcycle-related features.

This is the author's fourth motorcycling book, reflecting his declared admiration for BMW's unique and original engineering approach, and the company's willingness to risk entirely new ideas.